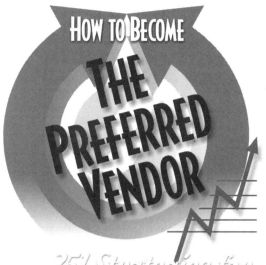

HOW TO BECOME

THE PREFERRED VENDOR

251 Strategies for Doing More Business with Retailers!

D1611745

HOW TO BECOME

THE PREFERRED VENDOR

251 Strategies for Doing More Business with Retailers!

Rick Segel & Tom Shay

Specific House

How To Become The Preferred Vendor

251 Strategies for Doing More Business with Retailers!

Published by:

Specific House Publishing
One Wheatland Street
Specific House Burlington, MA 01803

Specific House Publishing
One Wheatland St.
Burlington, MA 01803
781-272-9995
781-272-9996 (fax)

Printed in the United States of America

ISBN: 0-9674586-2-5

TABLE OF CONTENTS

DEDICATIONS

From Rick Segel:

I would like to dedicate this book to all those vendors and manufacturers who work hard every day to improve the lives of retailers. You are the resources who understand that supplying goods or services to a retailer is a partnership. You know that being a good partner means working at the relationship, always looking for new ideas and finding the courage to keep trying them.

To the newest members of my family—Shawn Ryan Osborne and Alexis Sara Freson, my new grandchildren—I also dedicate this book so they will some day know that their grandparents tried to make a difference in the world and make it just a little better place for us all to live in. That commitment is part of who my grandchildren are and what they will become.

To my wife, partner, soul mate, lover, and best friend, Margie—who shares in all of the work but rarely gets the credit—I dedicate this book and every book I will ever write. Margie is the person behind the scenes, the director, producer, critic, and encourager. She is the one who makes it all possible, without pomp or flair but with a quiet (sometimes not so quiet) "let's make it work" approach that helps me turn ideas into dreams and dreams into reality.

From Tom Shay:

The first sales representative I remember was Mr. O.C. North. He called on my grandfather representing Big Smith of Carthage, Missouri. As I grew up, I knew Mr. and Mrs. North as neighbors. Their daughter Marilyn was my first baby sitter. Over the years as my father had his own stores, Mr. North, and later his son, John Paul North, called on my father. Mr. North was the first in a long line of quality sales representatives who called on our stores for the next 40 years. However, Mr. North was neither the first nor the last of the sales representatives who consider the buyers they call on as friends. To these people I dedicate this book.

Many people helped to shape the experiences I drew upon in writing this book: my grandparents, Verna and Buster Brown; my parents, Shirley and Frank Shay; and those individuals who chose to work in our family businesses. They shared their knowledge, their kindness, and a positive attitude—all so important to me.

Another group I acknowledge are those many retailers who have been so kind as to be part of my retail experience in recent years. They have heard my presentations, read my magazine articles, and read the books I wrote. To them, I dedicate this book, because it has been written with the intent of helping them become more profitable in their business and better enjoy this wonderful industry we are all in. These fine people represent the future of retail.

Preface

Rick Segel and Tom Shay think like retailers, act like retailers, and understand the highs and lows a retailer feels. The reason is that they share more than 50 years of front line retail experience, having owned retail stores and been brought up in retail families. But that's where the similarities end. Tom comes from Arkansas with a department and hardware store background, whereas Rick is from Boston with 25 years' experience in specialty retailing, as owner of one of New England's most successful independent women's specialty stores.

During their retailing careers, both Tom and Rick were invited to write articles for a number of trade publications—invitations that eventually gave birth to independent writing, speaking, and consulting careers. These career paths started to cross at various trade shows where both were speaking. Coincidentally, as the two seasoned presenters compared stories about their more than 2,000 appearances all over the world, a similar theme began to emerge. It was hidden in a question asked of each speaker at almost every trade show. Significantly, this recurring question was being asked not by the retailers Rick and Tom were hired to address at the trade shows, but by the sales reps and manufacturers who were exhibiting there.

The question always began in a similar fashion with a rhetorical "You were a retailer" or "You talk to retailers all the time." Then came the real question:

"How can I do more business with them?"

Each time, the questioner quickly added the qualifier:

"That's without giving it away."

Translation: How can I increase my business with retailers without reducing my prices?

As Rick and Tom shared with each other the solutions they recommended in responding to the sales reps and manufacturers, they came to realize that even the most basic suggestion they offered was received with amazement.

Typical response: "I never thought of that!"

This nearly universal thirst for common solutions gave rise to *How to Become the Preferred Vendor.*

This book is a collection of those solutions—each one a tested idea that really works.

The purpose of this book, however, is not to present detailed, in-depth recipes stating exactly how to do what and when. We respect your professionalism too much to tell you how to implement the obvious. Instead, our purpose is to be a solid source of ideas, strategies, tactics, and concepts that you can adapt to the needs of your retailers, thereby repositioning you, the vendor, as a valued must-have resource in the eyes of your customers.

As we circulated drafts of *How to Become the Preferred Vendor* to sales reps for preliminary feedback, we discovered that our ideas got our readers' creative juices flowing, and they began using these ideas immediately.

The strategy each vendor actually used had its roots in one of our ideas, but it was his or her own creation. We say that because the expression we hear most often after someone reads this book is:

"We took your idea on _____ and added _____ or changed _____ and it worked perfectly for us. Thanks for the idea."

At first we thought this outcome was not good. But soon we realized that our main purpose was met—to stimulate thought. As one manufacturer told Rick, "Your ideas got me thinking the right way, and I had the solution I needed in no time." That is why we purposely made this book and its recommendations as user-friendly as possible, keeping each idea short, to the point, and workable.

Stimulating thought is the ultimate goal of education. And an important premise behind this book is the power of education. People like to do business with those who know what they are talking about. For one thing, your ability to give retailers needed information and expertise deflects attention away from price. For another, today's need for expertise is greater than ever. There is so much to learn to keep up in the industry.

But the main reason we want to share *How To Become the Preferred Vendor* with you is that vendors and industries that adopt a pro-education agenda toward their market are always the winners and leaders.

We hope you are inspired to the point of adopting several of our ideas for reaching your market more effectively, thereby enabling your retailers to reach their markets. Transform these ideas, change them, disagree with them—but at least consider them, because they have the potential to change your business forever. We challenge you to greatness. In return, if we inspire a great idea, please pass that along to us. (The back of this book tells you how to get in touch with us.)

Enjoy, and keep working to improve your business and the business of your retailers.

ADVERTISING–
IT'S MORE
THAN CO-OP!

ADVERTISING–
IT'S MORE THAN CO-OP!

Introduction

Gurus tell us to think out of the box. We've also heard that there's more than one way to skin a cat. Both expressions mean the same thing: we can't do things the way we have always done them.

This portion of the book explores unique, interesting, and different tactics that you can adopt and adapt to WOW your retailers and make their registers ring, putting you on the path of being the preferred resource.

1.
Become the Ad Librarian—Collect Ads for Retailers

You can become the source of advertising ideas for your retailers. Collect ads from your accounts and create a library of advertising. Try to get comments from those retailers about how well each ad worked. Make note of the type of store, the medium (local newspapers, magazines, radio, or TV spot), and why it worked or didn't. Knowing why an ad didn't work can be just as important as why it did!

You can place your collection of ads and notes on your company web site in a section for retailers. The collection also makes great content for a print or electronic newsletter (e-zine) or even as an advertisement to send people to your web site.

2.
Add Other Industries to Your Library

Look for great advertising from other industries that can be adapted to retail. Create a library of interesting ad concepts. It's even okay to collect actual advertising from other industries and block out the names of the stores and then put these into e-zines, newsletters, and/or web sites.

. . . .

Dewars Scotch ran an ad concept for years in which it profiled people who liked Dewars. The ads featured photos of the individuals and gave some personal information about them, including the fact that their favorite store was the one running the ad.

. . . .

3.
Create Ads Your Retailers Can Use

This idea has been around for years, but one problem is that the ads become stale. Another problem is that these ads have traditionally been institutional ads for the manufacturers, without doing much for the stores. Ads you create for your retailers must be store-focused, with the ability to feature the <u>business</u> as well as the benefits of the <u>product</u>. These ads must be proven winners and state-of-the art, offering the flexibility for local adjustments.

4.
Be the Source—
Supply Photos and Logos

A great format for cable TV is a store's presentation of a series of photos that change every six seconds, with a musical background and a voice-over. But photos are expensive for an individual retailer to produce, whereas most manufacturers already have files of high-quality photos, which enable the retailer to meet cable TV's required production quality.

Photos and logos can also be used for a store's web site, magazine ads, brochures, direct mail pieces, and of course newspaper ads. Supplying these resources costs you, the manufacturer or vendor, very little, especially if the photos are made available in 72 dpi and 300 dpi in a section of your web site that is easily downloadable. Retailers will appreciate this service and will prefer buying from you simply because you are supplying the photos. You gain a competitive advantage with very little work.

5.
Cut Through Red Tape—Offer Retailer-Friendly Co-op Advertising

Co-op advertising has been around for years, but the biggest problem for retailers is filling out the forms and meeting all the requirements to get co-op money. After that's done they have to wait a long time to get a check. Most retailers feel as if it's not worth the effort.

If you want an effective co-op ad program that is used, streamline the process. Allow a retailer to apply for co-op fund reimbursement without requiring advance approval. Fast-track the procedure by making the approval process take only one day or, even better, three hours. Allow the retailer to fax the ad to you with a simple form stating costs and placement, and then issue an immediate credit against any existing invoices. Some vendors prefer issuing credit while others prefer checks. And some give checkbooks to their sales reps to speed up the process even more.

6.

Promote Store-Focused Co-op Advertising

To help build both the store's business and your own, allow the retailer's name to be the most prominent name appearing in the ads. Too often a vendor's co-op restrictions wind up creating an ad that resembles a dealer-listing ad. Remember that the retailer pays a substantial part of the advertising cost. You want the consumer to go to that particular store to look for the merchandise—not to just any store. If retailers cannot reap the benefits of their own ads, they are going to stop participating in your co-op program.

7.

It's a High-Tech World— Allow On-line Processing

To further streamline the process of reimbursing co-op advertising claims, let your retailers complete co-op advertising forms on-line and invite them to attach a scanned copy of the ad and the newspaper invoice.

8.
And the Winner Is—
Your Annual Advertising Contest

Sponsor an advertising competition that encourages retailers to advertise your products—and at the same time that generates great advertising ideas you can use in becoming a valued resource. People are motivated by competition; plus, retailers enjoy saying they have "award winning" advertising. Judge the ads on originality of concept, construction of the ad, and any other considerations you deem important.

Four keys to great advertising contests:

➤ Make it easy for retailers to enter.

➤ Categorize entries by size of the store so the smaller stores have a chance at winning in their size category.

➤ Make the prize worth the effort. You want to give a significant cash prize but you also want to award a nice plaque or trophy for the store to display for its customers to see.

➤ Create a strong public relations initiative, with press releases submitted to trade publications. Some vendors advertise pictures of the winners with their trophies or checks.

9.
What a Way to Get Ideas— Have a Sale Competition

Competition doesn't have to be limited to advertising. Ideas for sales are just as valuable. The biggest problem in retailing is that most retailers don't know how to run a sale properly. (No one goes to "sale school.") That is why you want to look not only for great sale ideas but also for effective procedures and timing. The more details you can gather about a successful sale, the more valuable this information becomes. In addition to requesting samples of the ads, have your entry requirements ask about store layout, signage, staffing, employee and customer contests, themes, employee meetings, sales performance, and advertising.

10.
The Winner Again—
Have a Sign Competition

Great signage has built many retail businesses. Some retailers have built entire businesses around effective signage and billboards. Clever phrases get customers talking about a business, and that becomes word-of-mouth advertising—the best form of advertising there is.

A fitness center built a multimillion-dollar business with one rather off-beat sign that asked:

Are You Fat and Ugly?
Would You Just Like to be Ugly?
Come to the West End Gym.

11.
Share What You Learned— Toot Your Own Horn

The value to you of any type of competition is the chance to share the winning ideas with other retailers of your products, to acknowledge the winners, and to "raise the bar" in your industry. Print either the winning concepts or all the entries in a book or booklet to give away to all your retailers. The number of entries will determine the size of what you publish and how often you choose to publish it.

12.
Supply the Signage

It's easy to give ideas for signage, but supplying good Point-of-Purchase signs always helps sell merchandise. This idea has been around for years, but you can put a different twist on it by furnishing creative tips on how to use the signs, where to put them, and what kind of positive effect the signage should or could have on the store's business. Develop signs with enough flexibility to incorporate the store's logo as well as your own.

13.
It's All About Ideas—
Offer Sign Concepts and Ideas

The easiest way to become a sign resource for your retailers is to devote a section of your web site to professionally designed store signs. These could be easily downloaded full sized. The difference between this idea and the preceding one is that you are not printing the signs. The retailer does the actual printing.

An interesting twist is to allow the retailer to sketch a sign, fax it to you, and have your graphic designer recreate it in Adobe PDF (portable document format) down-loadable by the retailer.

14.
Athletes Have Them, Why Not You? An Ad Coach

Ideas are great but getting people to act on them is something else. Coaching is growing in popularity in all aspects of business. So offer a service—for a minimal fee—whereby an advertising coach talks to the retailer for 30 minutes every week or every other week. The purpose of each coaching session is to ensure that the ideas the retailer likes are acted on—the friendly reminder we all need at times. Coaches don't have to be advertising or design specialists as long as they are understanding individuals with a basic comprehension of marketing and what the retailer is trying to accomplish. The growing popularity of coaching has increased the number and types of coaches available today. A web search will uncover an abundance of qualified coaches— a less-expensive method than the use of internal personnel.

15.

Offer a Monthly Advertising Service that Provides Ads

This is a service in which you send retailers advertising ideas, copy, concepts, and actual ads. The most cost-efficient way of doing so today is via your web site, but e-mail and old-fashioned mail work just fine. Include ad ideas from other industries. Some vendors charge their retailers a nominal fee for the service; however, your retailers will be far more impressed if it's an add-on you provide free.

16.

It's Cheap, So Why Not Create an Advertising E-zine?

Send your retailers a weekly e-mail of helpful tips, tools, and resources about retail advertising. These e-mails don't have to be lengthy; in fact, they are more effective when short and to the point. The weekly contact puts your company name in front of your customers even if they don't use any of the ideas. Just the fact that you are offering the ideas goes a long way toward keeping you in the mind of each retailer.

17.

Best Business-Building Ad—
Offer a "Q&A" Ad Service

The question-and-answer ad format is one of the most successful advertising concepts ever created. It is used successfully by many different types of retailers over a long term.

Let's first define the Q&A ad. It is a series of single column, 4-inch-long ads that run in local newspapers once a week, 52 weeks a year. The headline remains a consistent "Ask The Gift Expert"— or whatever subject you are the expert about. A small picture or caricature sketch of the owner or manager of the retail business is included, along with his or her name and a title, such as giftware expert or professional. A short question is followed by an answer. At the bottom of the ad is the store logo.

Where you, the manufacturer, play a part is to introduce the concept to one retailer in each media market and help develop the questions and answers. This type of advertising builds your retailer's brand (as well as your own) and positions each retailer as the expert. It also positions your company as an authority in your industry. You become the source for the retailing experts.

28

18.

Keep Them Advertising—
The Power of the Ad Budget

Getting retailers to budget for their advertising spending is one of the most challenging jobs for any consultant. Whatever help you can offer will go a long way toward establishing you with your retailers.

You can accomplish this educational task in several ways: by producing an informative booklet, creating a section on your web site, setting up a teleconference, or organizing a live seminar (for which you can charge a registration fee and introduce other ideas you are gaining from this book).

Promote these benefits of ad budgeting:

➤ Retailers save money by negotiating more favorable media rates for total yearly expenditures rather than for short-term spurts.

➤ Retailers increase their name recognition from the proven repetitions that a long-term commitment to advertising makes possible.

➤ Retailers streamline their buying patterns, since long-term advertising focuses them on the merchandise needed to back up a long-term ad campaign.

19.
Host an Advertising Hotline

This service offers an 800 number for your retailers to call for advice and answers to their advertising questions. Enhance this idea by inviting retailers to send you a videotape, audiotape, or fax of their ads and supporting materials, and having one of your staff assist the retailer in resolving problems. A retailer could also forward a media contract before signing it so a staff person could check the contract rate against established media guides.

This kind of service does not require internal staffing; it can be outsourced for a more cost-efficient result.

20.
Offer a Proofing Service for Ads

Invite retailers to fax each ad proof to one of your eagle-eyed staffers so it can be reviewed quickly for accuracy and completeness before the retailer approves its release to the media.

21.

Be the Expert—Have a Sale Helpline

Running a sale is a specialized skill that requires professional expertise. The problem is that professionals can be expensive, which almost defeats the purpose of running the sale. Having a help line to assist your retailers run sales can pay huge dividends.

If you don't have someone capable of providing such advice, subcontract the work to an expert who will return calls to retailers within 12 hours. A sale helpline is a wonderful service that retailers will greatly appreciate.

22.

Let's Talk—Create an Advertising Chat Room or Bulletin Board

An effective way to get retailers to keep visiting your web site is to create a chat room or on-line discussion bulletin board that focuses on retailers exchanging experiences and questions about advertising.

Allow enough time to develop these features so they work smoothly.

23.
Let's Get Together—Create a Retail Advertising Advisory Panel

Ask a select group of blue-ribbon retailers, key salespeople, marketing personnel, and production people to meet once a year to discuss issues of advertising. The panel's agenda should include issues and trends that affect the industry, retailers, manufacturing, and wholesaling. Such meetings generally take place at trade shows (see Tip #177), with results published in company newsletters. The goal for a program such as this is to increase the efficiency of everyone's advertising investments.

24.
Get a Ringer on the Team— Put an Ad Pro on Your Panel

Make sure you have an advertising professional on your retail advisory panel to ensure that when the ideas start flying around, they are doable. You don't want to end a meeting with, "I'll have to check to see if advertising can do that." Try to have someone from your ad department on the panel, but if you can attract an advertising pro who doesn't work for you to attend these meetings, even better. An outside voice brings no preconceived beliefs to say "That was tried in the past."

25.
Use an Experienced Facilitator

Make sure your advisory panel has a facilitator who knows how to direct a meeting, keep it running, and see that everybody contributes—not just a few dominant voices. The facilitator should have an agenda and make sure the meeting stays on task and on time. These sessions should be recorded and transcribed at a later time.

26.
Promote by Fax—Why Not, Everyone Else is Sending E-mail!

With the advent of e-mail, the fax has been relegated to a second-class means of communication. That means fax traffic is down and the probability of your messages being read is up. Whereas e-mails are easily deleted, faxes aren't.

Use a fax to send retailers a copy of an ad they can use to promote your products. Code the bottom section of the paper so it carries each retailer's account number. Invite the recipients to order a supply of these printed ads by filling in a quantity and faxing it back. You'll send the necessary advertising slicks and signage with the order. This is a practical method for merchandise ordered a season in advance as well as merchandise that is available on short notice.

27.
Offer Pictures, Logos, and Content on Your Web Site

The web is a powerful tool in the area of advertising. Many of the ideas you are reading about in just the advertising section of this book did not exist five years ago. Today, making resources available for downloading is one of the most empowering concepts around. Currently it is being practiced in the home appliance industry.

By making a variety of pictures, logos, and text available to your retailers on a password-protected section of your web site, you make it easy for them to create their own high-quality, customized ads, flyers, and brochures. They choose what merchandise they want to feature and the related text and pictures they favor. Then—like playing with paper dolls—they simply cut and paste. You can also store the retailers' own logos on your site to complete the ad.

We believe this one-stop do-it-yourself approach is the future of co-op advertising.

28.
Plan, Plan, Plan— Create an Advertising Workbook

Retailers too often place their advertising week to week. But if you develop a workbook, you can assist the retailer in planning ads for the quarters of the year—and budgeting accordingly. Also offer seasonal ideas for ads and promotions.

29.
Put the Advertising Workbook On-line

Create a place on your web site where retailers can access the ad workbook and budget planning device. Select a common format, such as a customized Excel spreadsheet or interactive web page, which allows retailers to input their last 12-month sales history or future sales goals. Have the budget planning device ask what percentage of their sales they want to allocate to advertising and what media they want to use. Individual retailers could maintain their information securely on your web site if you make each record password-protected.

30.
A Little Incentive—
Pay Retailers for Advertising Results

Offer an incentive in the form of credit or cash to retailers who furnish you with an advertising response report. Have them include a copy of the ad with a form that addresses these factors:

➤ Info about how the ad pulled

➤ Pictures of how the merchandise was displayed

➤ Examples of signage

➤ Sell-through

➤ Weather and any community activities taking place during the run of the ad

➤ Interesting anecdotes

You must ask the retailers if they want this information shared with others. Some will be glad to share while others will want the name of their store withheld.

A little incentive goes a long way.

31.
Success Sells—
Share Advertising Success Stories

Use a printed newsletter, on-line newsletter, or e-zine to tell retailers about the successes others have had advertising your merchandise. Include photos, testimonials, and stories of unique experiences with customers. Testimonials and referrals are the best form of advertising, and this sharing concept encourages more of it.

32.
Develop a Postcard Reminder Series

Retailers are busier than ever, so save their time by reaching them with a short message—the postcard. Used in a series, postcards can remind retailers of your advertising resources, toll-free helpline, an upcoming conference or trade show, or a series of helpful hints on how to improve their business. Here's one source of postcards to get you started: www.modernpostcard.com

33.
Be Creative—Reward Sales Reps for Orders with Ad Plans

Stores that advertise your product will sell more of it. So focus the retailer on advertising your product and enjoy a win/win for everyone. Create a bonus for your sales reps who write orders that have ad plans attached. Further reward those reps who follow through, with bonuses paid only on the completion of the plan.

To be eligible, a sales rep's order should be accompanied by an advertising plan, display plan, signage plan, and a request for any necessary support material from the manufacturer.

34.
Make it Easy to Show Your Stuff— Supply Display Props

Mannequins, backdrops, build-ups, lamps, illuminated signage, and other display props are great ways to cement in the customer's mind the branding of both the retail store and your products—especially when the props you supply already bear your logo, company name, or other identifiers.

35.
It's Worked for Years— Exterior Signage

Everyone remembers the Coca-Cola signs of years ago that hung over small storefronts. Today, many small retailers on a budget will allow you to do the same thing: co-brand with them for the signage that appears outside their building or on the signboard at a shopping center.

36.
Make Them the Star— Feature a Retailer in Your Advertising

When you advertise your products in trade magazines, feature one of your better retailers giving a testimonial about the profitability and sell-through of your products. Be sure the ad profiles the retailer. Frame a copy of the ad and deliver it to the retailer.

TEACH THEM TO FISH– EDUCATIONAL OPPORTUNITIES

TEACH THEM TO FISH–
EDUCATIONAL OPPORTUNITIES

Introduction

B usinesses are starting to realize that education is one of the most powerful armaments in their arsenal of marketing weapons. Offering knowledge and skills that improve the lives or the businesses of your clients or customers is one of the fastest ways to increase your own business.

➤ First, there is more business to be had by everyone.

➤ Second, sharing the same knowledge with others gets more people beginning to think the same way.

➤ Third, you are remembered, because people rarely forget those who change their way of thinking.

This second part of *How to Become the Preferred Vendor* is divided into two sections:

Section A. How to Educate

Section B. What Topics to Cover

Section A.
How to Educate

You have multiple ways of distributing information today, from methods as basic as a sales rep's sharing an idea with a retailer in person, to using any number of forms of electronic transfer, such as by producing a newsletter. Whatever methods you use for educating your retailers, they will perceive you as someone who cares—which helps develop trust between you.

Here are some of the ways to carry out your educational objectives.

37.
Offer Workshops and Bring Your Retailers Together

Host a conference or symposium and invite some of your better retailers to be speakers. They will be honored to attend, and you will discover some great new ideas that you can share with more retailers through post-conference newsletters.

Offer a variety of programs at all levels of expertise, including some basic skills—for example, basic advertising. Even the most experienced retailers might not have taken an advertising course before, and they'll gain new insight. And for those who do know their basics, reviewing them can reinforce why those retailers are successful and why they do what they do so well.

38.
Start a "Recommended Reading" List

Review the best retail books available and write your own reviews of them. Suggest the best chapters and explain why you like them so much. Invite your retailers to suggest their own candidates for the list.

39.
Offer Teleseminars for Your Retailers

A twist on the teleconference is the seminar or workshop that uses a telephone bridge line. Because this technology is relatively new, you may have to oversimplify the process so your retailers feel comfortable about taking advantage of your teleseminars.

You can offer a variety of classes from beginning advertising to more advanced topics.

Pick one night a month to hold classes, preferably Mondays, Tuesdays, or Wednesdays. Supply a handout in Adobe PDF (portable document format) that retailers can download from your web site and read—or print—no matter what kind of computers they use.

40.
Teleseminars with Visuals

Webex and other web sites are available today that allow you to hold meetings on-line with graphics. The concept uses telephone bridge lines so a number of people can call in on the same line and all can view a PowerPoint graphic presentation. It's a 21st-century way of having a meeting without leaving the store.

41.
Create Quizzes or Tests on Your Web site

Add a multiple choice quiz to your web site to further involve your re-tailers in learning while enjoying the competitive spirit. Be sure to change the content on a regular basis to encourage repeat visits.

42.
Build a Tool for Learning

Consider building a business tool that will help retailers run their businesses, as Tom Shay has done on his web site, www.profitsplus.org Retailers enter their own financial data into a secure area. The format enables small businesses to calculate their information, thereby gaining greater insight into their own store's direction.

43.
Offer Tutorial Courses– Electronically

Contract with a training professional to create 20-minute presentations on topics of importance, and make these available in audio or video in CD, DVD, or VHS formats. Add a workbook containing self-tests so retailers can see how well they are mastering each topic.

These audio or video presentations could be given away as an incentive or a bonus—such as for placing an order or visiting your booth at trade show. They can also be sold.

44.
A Clipping Service and You

Contract with a clipping bureau to send copies of ads from other retailers to your accounts. Clipping services also provide composite reports of the print ads within a particular industry. Add your commentary about the ads to assist your retailers in learning how other businesses are advertising.

45.
Suggestion Book for Displays

Equip your sales representatives with booklets that suggest ways of displaying your merchandise. Include photos and step-by-step guides so retailers can see how to mount these displays.

46.
Reps Are Teachers Too!

Offer to have your sales representatives hold after-hours classes for retailers and their staff. Retailers will appreciate your reducing the amount of training they have to provide to all new hires.

➤ Certain skills, such as how retailers can improve their customer service, are more effectively taught face to face than by simply saying that customer service needs to be improved.

➤ Other skills are more suited for computer-based learning—including skills developed by implementing many of the ideas in this book—and thereby reduce travel issues.

To encourage your sales force's participation, offer them financial incentives. And to build their confidence for conducting classes for retailers, also offer them train-the-trainer learning from professionals.

47.
Surveys Give as Well as Get Information

As a manufacturer, distributor, or wholesaler, you are in a unique position to poll your retailers' opinions and experiences—from a simple "How's business?" to the specific "What percentage of your sales do you spend on advertising or payroll?" The enticement to respond to a survey is that the retailer gets a detailed report on the results. All retailers want to know how their neighbors are doing and how they stack up in comparison.

Surveys can be taken via e-mail, mail, fax, or telephone. Many vendors have built businesses by getting a reputation for conducting annual surveys that provide valuable results to the retailer—and to you, as well, because the information can be submitted to the press, both general and trade. This positions you, the vendor, as an authority within your industry—a hidden benefit of becoming known for your surveys.

As the ad says, try it—you'll like it.

48.

A Different Kind of Survey— Advertising Costs

Instead of surveying retailers, you can do as some companies do for their customers: research costs of resources that you'd like to encourage your retailers to use. Conduct a survey of advertising costs, for instance. Our experience tells us that many retailers shy away from different advertising methods because they don't know what the costs are or make false assumptions about them. Learning the approximate range of rates charged by graphic designers, ad agencies, newspapers, magazines, radio, and TV can overcome a retailer's hesitation to try new media.

Gathering this information is not as difficult as you might think; every professional association polls its members on similar questions. You might find the information by simply researching the Internet and requesting permission to use the findings.

49.
Share the Success Stories

Retailers want to know what works and what doesn't work. But because e-commerce is still a relatively new concept for many retailers, they are not likely to use its advantages to search for successful models. Retailers will beat a path to your door if you discover and collect these models from your retail accounts and share them with other retailers.

Collect these success stories in a special section of your web site. Include them in your newsletter, both printed and electronic. Share them with your sales reps and encourage them to share the models with their retailers. This kind of knowledge will make you a resource for your retailers and establish you as a guide to e-zine success.

50.
Easy Education—
Turn out a Tips Booklet

Tips booklets are easy to create and use, filled with facts, not fluff. They can cover any aspect of retail business management such as advertising, store layout, display, personnel, and staff meetings.

They are typically not more than about 20 pages and measure 5-1/2" by 8-1/2". Another trend in publishing is toward the tall and narrow pocket-sized booklet, 8-1/2" by 3-3/4".

51.
Different from a Conference or Symposium—Retail Retreats

There's no better way to get closer to your accounts than to host a retreat where retailer and vendor are together for a two-day period. Retreats can vary in purpose from all educational to a combination of education and networking or education and buying. There's a growing trend among vendors whose lines are big enough to hold their own mini-trade shows instead of participating in major trade shows. They invite key retailers to an all-expense-paid retreat (except for airfare), having determined that the costs of covering lodging, ground transportation, food, drinks, and seminars for the retailers, added to the loss of exposure at a major trade show, are more than justified by the increased size of orders written as a result of the retreat and the strong relationships formed during the two days together.

Section B.
What Topics to Cover

Information about the following topics can serve as content for your web site, newsletter, and e-zine, but we believe that a tips book is the fastest and easiest way to position yourself as the concerned partner and resource for your retailers.

52.
Best Ways to Negotiate Ad Rates

Have one of your staff do the research or hire an advertising professional to write the content for you that tells how to negotiate the best deals with newspapers, magazines, and radio and TV stations. Include the highlights of interviews with sales managers and salespeople from the different media talking about the best ways to get the best deals, and include examples.

53.
Best Ways to Advertise Your Products

Position yourself head and shoulders above your competition by taking the time to develop your own theories on advertising and putting them in writing. Work with your ad agency, writer, editor, and graphics designer, or find a publications coordinator to help you produce a book that can be distributed to your accounts. (Don't be reluctant to distribute the book to those who are not your accounts—they just might become an account after seeing a well-done educational tool such as your book.) The process is not as difficult as it may seem. If you contact either Rick or Tom, we will be happy to help you with this project.

54.
Image Advertising or Price Item Advertising?

The topic of price item advertising versus image advertising has been debated for years. The purpose of your tips booklet is to explain the rationale behind each type of advertising—an excellent opportunity to demonstrate how your products are being advertised both ways.

55.
Billboards–The Great Confusion

Billboards are one of the most misunderstood advertising vehicles for smaller retailers. Billboards build brands and successful brands build businesses. Teaching retailers how to use a billboard effectively can help them break out of the "constant sale" mentality.

This topic is one of the easier to develop with a tips booklet or book, because suppliers of billboards are more than happy to cosponsor with you and provide all the information you need.

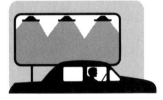

56.
Building the Trust Customer

The Trust Customer is the buyer who is willing to spend more money for an item because he or she has developed trust in the retailer. Many stores build their entire business around this type of customer. Instead of focusing on ways they can reduce price by 20 percent, they focus on ways they can increase the price by 20 percent. You can create a tips book explaining in a concise format the ways that successful retailers build trust with their customers, how they advertise, and how they build their brand.

57.
Nontraditional Means of Advertising

Newspaper, radio, TV, and other traditional forms of advertising are not the retailer's only options for drawing customers. No-cost or low-cost ideas for boosting traffic are available. For example, getting a new customer into the store for the first time is an expensive proposition. But getting existing customers, who are often ignored, to come into the store for a specific reason is an effective strategy—one you can describe in detail in a tips booklet that will be much appreciated by the retailer.

• •

One appliance retailer's calls to 10 existing customers a day resulted in a sales conversion rate of 16 percent. Even more impressive was this retailer's ability to:

➤ recognize that problems existed for 2 percent of those customers, and

➤ take steps to correct the situation.

It's hard to resolve a problem unless you know the problem exists. This telephoning tactic increased the retailer's sales and saved customers.

And sharing this kind of tip with your retailers can increase your value as a vendor.

• •

58.

Merchandise Compatibility— No Brand is an Island

Retailers are often guilty of carrying high-quality product lines in one part of their business and low-quality items when it comes to the accessories. Great brands have died in good stores because they did not have a strong supporting cast. A useful topic to cover in a small four-page brochure informs your retailers of the other product lines that perform well together with your brand. So if you want your merchandise to do better on the selling floor, provide the details about the other lines that complement your line.

59.

Solving the Mystery—Open To Buy

One of the more difficult concepts for smaller retailers to understand and implement is "Open to Buy." Traditionally it is one of the most requested seminars at trade shows. Because you know what it means, it gives you a much-needed teaching opportunity to help your retailers. You can offer the learning in the form of a tips book, teleseminar, trade-show-sponsored seminar, suggested readings, or a web site demonstration, such as the one Tom has at www.profitsplus.org, where a free open-to-buy calculator can be downloaded.

60.
Share the Best of Cable TV Techniques

Good concepts in cable TV advertising are worth a fortune. Unfortunately, many independent retailers are not aware of them. They depend on the expertise of the local cable company, which is generally very limited. To help your retailers use cable TV effectively, find the stores that use this medium most successfully and ask for a copy of their tape. They are usually more than willing to share.

Collect all the do's and don'ts about cable advertising in the format of a tips book. Also create a video library of cable TV ads that could be compiled into one long-playing presentation of ads, accompanied by a separate worksheet that gives a thumbnail description of the purpose of the ad and its track record.

In 1993, Rick Segel's retail store was one of the three finalists in a cable TV awards program competing against almost 5,000 entries from all over the country. He was nominated because of the concept and style he used in the ad. The sad part of the story is that no one other than the station rep and Rick knew about the concept or the reason for it—a waste of valuable information. It would have been much more beneficial to the other entrants if the ad concept had been highlighted as the winning technique.

When you educate your retailers by creating materials that feature examples of good ads, be sure to document the purpose of each.

61.
Cash Flow Management—Ways to Get Involved

If you are offering dating terms of payment on your invoices, assist the retailer in understanding cash flow management. Many retailers become overextended because of the buy now / sell later / and pay much later syndrome.

62.
Elements of a Winning Promotion

Develop a checklist of all the elements needed to create a great promotion. This can be as simple as a small brochure or as ambitious as a multipage checklist that includes a detailed explanation of what each element represents.

PART 3

PROMOTIONS– IT'S MORE THAN PRICE

PROMOTIONS–
IT'S MORE THAN PRICE

Introduction

"Highlighting, spotlighting, focusing, or bringing to the attention of," are the words the dictionary uses to define the terms <u>promote</u>, <u>promoting</u> and <u>promotion</u>. True, price is one way to bring attention, but it's only one way. Here are tips for <u>non</u>–sale-price promotions that can spotlight, focus, and bring lots of attention to your business without your giving any money away.

63.
Promotion Doesn't Mean Sale!

Promotions do not have to represent price reductions. Manufacturers should change their focus from price to the excitement of the product or promotion. Let's learn from the movie industry. *Harry Potter* reached $200 million in revenue in two weeks, even though the whole world knew the film could be seen soon enough on a $3 rental video—and the neighborhood could be invited in to see it for the same $3. Despite the known 90 percent price reduction, people turned out at full price because of the buzz and excitement generated by all the hoopla.

64.
Use a Book as a Promotional Offer

If you use any direct mail and you are looking for an immediate response from retailers, include an offer that will require retailers to take action before an expiration date. A promotion used very successfully by many vendors is the offer of a free book.

One vendor purchased 1,000 copies of Rick Segel's *Retail Business Kit for Dummies* to use as an incentive for responding to the vendor's mailing. If you do business with other vendors who sell to retailers, just call Rick or Tom—they'll be more than happy to sell you multiple copies of this book.

65.

Teleconference to the Top

Technology offers a wonderful opportunity for your stores to talk to the president of your company, your designers, sales managers, and/or advertising executives on a quarterly or semiannual basis. Use teleconferencing! Announce each teleconference by sending your retailers a postcard, and have your sales reps and customer service department remind them of the upcoming event.

This concept is very successful and is now commonplace on Wall Street, where analysts are invited to a quarterly financial review and allowed to ask questions. The real benefit from teleconferences is that it brings the retailer closer and more involved with your company, thereby helping you build lasting relationships.

66.

Sharing Hot Tips– Putting Success Stories to Work

Maintain a file of advertising success stories so that when you receive an order from a sales rep for a particular item, you can send a postcard or note to the retailer ahead of the order telling of the success of another retailer's advertising or promotion of that item

67.

Let Them Wear Your Name—An Alternative Outlet for Co-op Dollars

In addition to distributing earned co-op advertising money in traditional ways, offer an on-line catalog of company logo specialty items that retailers can order at large discounts, such as sweaters, polo shirts, mugs, and hats. Here are two benefits of such a program:

➤ The retailer has a way of rewarding staff.

➤ The smaller, loyal retailer has an incentive for using co-op advertising at any level.

Though small stores might say they do not want to waste their time doing co-op advertising to collect only $25, they might see greater value in collecting a sweater for a staff person that's worth much more.

68.

Wearing the Vendor's Name— Dressed to Sell

You can offer to your retailers a program whereby their employees can purchase signature clothing directly from the manufacturer. Almost every company today offers some type of shirt for its employees. Why not extend the idea to offer your retailers clothing to be worn at work at reduced prices—or even free? Signature clothing helps promote your product and makes the staff more aware of your merchandise.

An added twist is to get your apparel suppliers to offer their merchandise for the retail staff to wear on the sales floor.

69.

Create an Encyclopedia of Non-Sale Promotions

Start gathering examples of the best promotions that retailers have held to create excitement and sell merchandise without dropping prices.

70.
Make it Different—The Fun Fax

This is one of those ideas that not only your retailers should use in communicating with their customers but you, too, because the method works equally well to get a friendly image across in all your communications.

The concept is simple. Instead of sending a traditional or boring fax, spice it up with a cartoon or a few one-liners. Include the message, of course, but add the element of fun to the fax. It will get noticed and convey the message that you are approachable and fun to do business with—not to mention that this is the type of innovation people talk about. And if you want word-of-mouth advertising, give them something to talk about.

71.
Community Service Projects and Promotions

Staying involved in community service projects is an integral part of any retailer's marketing effort. Customers want to do business with people who care about their communities and the world around them. As a vendor, you might offer an award to your retailers for the best community service project. You can do so through state retail associations, many of which recognize retailers with award programs that are vendor-sponsored.

72.

Add a Best Promotion Page to Your Web Site

Start a collection of the best non-sale promotional events and display these on your web site for all your retailers to use. Make sure each event has a complete description that includes its title, theme, purpose, type of customer attracted, sales increases if any, increases to store's database, personnel required, and expenses. You want this to be a complete how-to library of promotional ideas.

73.

Encourage Retailers to Submit Promotions

Advertise and promote this collection of non-sale promotional events and offer incentives to your retailers to add their ideas. This can be accomplished via various contests, financial considerations, or just recognition. The goal is for you to get the reputation of providing a free service for your retailers to use.

74.
Help Retailers Create an Electronic Newsletter

E-zines are a new marketing tool that many retailers are still struggling with. If you publish a shell for them to use, your company name will be displayed as a sponsor—a constant source of advertising to their customers for very little money. Write most of the e-zine for your retailers and allow them to just plug in a story or ad in the format you created.

One inexpensive way of producing this e-zine is to form a strategic alliance with a company such as Microsoft's Bcentral.com, which publishes electronic newsletters. But many other smaller vendors can do just as good a job.

75.
Supply Press Releases for Your Retailers to Use

Instead of sending out a press release about one of your new products or lines—news that would rarely get local coverage—write a press release that incorporates the retailer. Either have your retailers send you a list of the local publications they would want it submitted to, or send a draft of the release to the retailers to further customize it and submit it themselves.

76.
Provide Page Content to Retailer's Web sites

The Internet is still in its infancy, and the ways retailers can use it are varied and almost unlimited. The Internet is a major area of opportunity for manufacturers to help retailers put together web sites or parts of web sites—and create win/win relationships. Many retailers have small web sites and don't have the money, time, or knowledge to devote to making the most of the web. This is where you can help by offering prepared pages for your retailers that work with their existing sites. Retailers gain quality pages and the manufacturer gets some inexpensive advertising.

77.
Create Press Release Templates for Your Retailers to Use

Create a simple template for a press release that reduces what the retailers have to do other than insert their store name, address, and a short, unique phrase describing the store. Offer different templates for announcing sales, new products, and new or retiring employees. Include a line that says "[ABC Retailer], carrying such famous brands as _____"—and fill in your brand's name.

78.

Collect Reasons for Having a Press Release

Press releases are a powerful marketing tool—if done properly. Collect reasons why and how your retailers can use press releases, and distribute the information via a section of your web site, an article in your newsletter or e-zine, or a tip in a booklet.

79.

Customer Appreciation Days— Not as Goofy as it Sounds

This overworked title is still very effective for many different types of retailers and vendors. Although some retailers look at Customer Appreciation Days as a meaningless cliché for just another promotion, others turn it into a major event and ask for vendor participation—which you can provide in the form of demonstrations, trunk shows, and free giveaway items, such as logo-imprinted merchandise. These events can result in major traffic- and revenue-producing opportunities. Track the industries that are successful and suggest the concept to your accounts. Generally, customer appreciation events create a true party atmosphere and include free refreshments. They have to be fun!

80.
Display Pros to the Rescue

Every retailer is on a constant, never-ending search for a way to display merchandise. Although larger stores have the buying power that gets their vendors to spend specialized one-on-one assistance, independent stores probably need the personalized assistance even more but are unable to get it. You can help with display ideas, techniques, workshops, or books of tips. Even photographs go a long way toward gaining your retailers' appreciation.

A manufacturer's supplying of props—free when possible or at a nominal fee when necessary—is also appreciated. Some manufacturers work out strategic alliances with various display supply houses to offer group discounts for specific items. But the simplest and most appreciated help can be to give retailers a list of sources where they can purchase the props and supplies.

81.
Show 'Em How to Show It!

You could offer to your retailers the services of a display specialist. This specialist would travel around to the stores primarily to help the retailer display the manufacturer's merchandise, but secondarily to offer some assistance with general display issues.

82.

Road Show—Staying in Touch

Create a road show between trade shows—a tradition that comes from the hardware industry. The field sales representatives present to retailers a small catalog of product offerings that have combinations of special dating, pricing, and delivery. This catalog is the "road show"—a great way to get some additional products and items into your accounts.

83.

Deals for Retailers

Offer price incentives to retailers who order seasonally instead of for at-once delivery.

84.
The Truckload Sale

This idea is popular among manufacturers in the power equipment trade. They load up an attractive truck with their merchandise and hold large parking lot sales together with their retailers—thereby saving the retailer from having to order all the items.

85.
The Trunk Show

As in the truckload sale, the manufacturer brings the merchandise to the retail store—but with the trunk show the sale takes place inside the store. In some cases, consumers place orders; in others, they take their purchases with them. Either way, the retailer pays only for the items ordered or sold, without being responsible for preordering all the merchandise. The benefit that the manufacturer provides is that the retailer receives the customer's money before having to pay the manufacturer—thereby making a profit and getting free financing.

86.

Keep Them Informed—What's New, What's Up, What's Happening?

Include in your newsletter or e-zine topical information about what's happening in your industry and with companies that affect your industry.

Smaller stores love to know what is happening at big stores: policy changes, gossip, management changes, or retail expansions.

87.

Start a Book Club

Offer retailers books on retail issues. Develop a form for them to sign up for your Book-of-the-Quarter Club and agree to be billed once a quarter. To the cover of each book, adhere a self-promotional sticker that identifies you as a vendor of choice.

88.

Who's the Ideal Customer– A Contest that Works for You

An interesting promotional idea that becomes a win/win for both you and your retailer is a contest to find the consumer who represents your product's ideal user. The idea comes from a promotion called "In Search of the Leslie Fay Woman" conducted by Leslie Fay, the woman's dress company. What the company was looking for was its ultimate loyal customer who loved the merchandise, used it, and was proud to be associated with it.

To enter the "In Search of the [Your Product Name] Person" contest, customers visit the store. The promotion works just as well for a range of products, from hardware to automobiles. It involves the retailer in encouraging its customers to enter. The cost is minimal because the prize winners receive merchandise. Other benefits of this promotion are that it helps both the manufacturer and retailer to define who their targeted customers are, and the retailer builds a mailing list for future promotions.

89.
The Packaging Difference— Your Packaging Counts

Impress your retailers by the way your merchandise is packaged when it is received at the store. Your professional image will in turn impress the ultimate consumer. The smallest things can sometimes have the biggest impact:

➤ Does the outside of your delivery box indicate quality and professionalism?

➤ Does the packaging tape have your logo on it?

➤ Does the box have your company name imprinted on it?

➤ When the UPS driver opens the truck, can the retailer immediately distinguish your packages among the hundreds of others?

➤ Is your image consistent—from the trade show experience to the receiving room to the sales floor to the customer's home?

90.
Leave a Paper Trail– Supply Ad Materials

Statement inserts and bag stuffers have been an advertising technique employed by manufacturers for years, and they are still effective promotional tools. Take the concept a step further by offering retailers a supply of basic capabilities brochures to place in strategic locations for consumers to pick up. A capabilities brochure is a pamphlet that contains a description and brief history of the store, what the store does, directions to it, type of merchandise carried—featuring yours, of course!—with your company name and a photograph of a piece of your merchandise. These trifold brochures begin with a single piece of 8-1/2" by 11" paper and a template for which the retailer supplies its logo, copy, and photographs.

The benefit of this promotion is that it cements the relationship between the store and the vendor: retailers continue to carry a line of merchandise that is named in their own brochures.

91.
The Shop in the Store

Many vendors have been successful in creating a shop-within-a-store in major department stores. However, this concept is ripe for smaller independents that have developed loyal followings for specific brands. Not limiting this type of marketing effort to the larger stores can significantly increase your sales.

92.
Grand Opening or Expansion Assistance

Any time that a store opens, expands, or has any type of special promotion, you have an opportunity to offer promotional items, merchandise, contest giveaways, imprinted bags, and refreshments. The goal is to be associated with the retailer from the onset of the relationship.

93.

Bring in the Reserves and Lend Extra Hands

During major events, grand openings, and other promotional events, retailers are hard pressed to find good sales floor staff. Retailers really appreciate extra sets of hands to supplement their own staff. Any way you can assist helps cement the relationship.

94.

How is Your Own Preferred Customer Program Working?

Preferred customer programs have become the #1 form of consumer direct mail advertising. The same concept works just as well between a vendor and a retailer. By knowing what your own customers' preferences are—down to the time they like to be called or what they like to buy— you can tap into this information resource to pinpoint your marketing efforts.

95.
Observe Frequency Incentives

You already know how important it is to reward your best customers—but your best customers are not necessarily the ones that spend the most money. Although the large retailer may spend a lot of money placing one order a year with you, the smaller retailer who consistently places small orders and who reorders weekly or monthly is considered by many to be the better customer. Be sure to reward your customers on the basis of their frequency of purchases.

96.
Go to the Top

Consider having an 800 phone number for retailers that plays a recorded message from the president of your company inviting the retailer to tell him or her the good, the bad, and the ugly—or to suggest how your company can improve. It would be a nice touch to have the president return each call, or return some calls on a random basis, although a special assistant to the president can contact the callers to thank them and ensure them that action will be taken on their comments.

97.
Retailing Scholarships

Numerous retail education formats are offered by specific trade associations, state associations, and the National Retail Federation. Show a retailer you really care by offering a free scholarship to attend one of these educational forums. This can be an annual award program announced at a trade show as well as through your web site, newsletters, and e-zines. Accompany this gesture with an adequate public relations effort that co-brands the local retailer with you and is promoted through the retailer's local newspaper. Make an investment in education.

98.
Free Samples?

Free works. It's how you can entice retailers to try out your merchandise. It is easy to say "no," but when handed something for nothing, no strings attached, it is difficult to turn it down. Sometimes all it takes to change a retailer's mind or attitude about a manufacturer and its merchandise is having the product in the store.

99.
It's More Than Just Cash

So far the retailer incentives we have been focusing on involve cash savings or additional merchandise. However, many vendors have opted to give prize incentives instead. One of the more popular is the ocean cruise, especially when the giveaway occurs on specific dates so that all the winners travel together and your key personnel can be aboard, too. One benefit of the vendor's presence is the ability to get to know the accounts better. Moreover, if any business is conducted, such as a retail educational seminar, it can make the trip tax deductible. Otherwise, recipients are legally obligated to pay taxes on the free trip.

100.
Send Airline Tickets

Select a retailer who never attends trade shows because of the cost, and offer a free airline ticket to attend a major trade show. You know that if the retailer were to see your complete product line or lines, you would completely justify the money spent. The other twist to this concept is to have two or three vendors used by the same retailer share the expense.

101.
Send a Needy Retailer to a Show (They're All Needy)

Reward your retailers for their purchases throughout the year by applying a percentage of their purchases toward the cost of their attending your annual trade show or conference. One wholesaler we know gives retailers individual certificates indicating how much of their hotel bill and meals have been prepaid. Of course, retailers can redeem their certificates only by attending the trade show, where they are highly likely to write additional purchase orders.

102.
"Frequent Buyer Smiles" for Different Levels of Customers

Some customers are more valuable than others, yet many vendors in retail have not figured this out or acknowledged their better customers. Other industries have, such as the airlines. By categorizing customers, they offer a platinum member more perks than a gold member. Thus, gold members work harder to earn the platinum level, know what they have to do to get there, and are motivated to stay with the same airline. You can recognize your retailers with a similar system. Most of them do not know how good an account they are for the vendor.

103.
Clubs: A New Item a Month

Many kinds of monthly buying programs are offered by vendors. The obvious benefit to the vendor is that new orders are generated every month. The benefit to the retailer is that fresh items are coming in monthly.

These automatic programs work in various ways. Some vendors introduce new styles or models—such as in apparel, collectable, and gift lines in which manufacturers are constantly adding new items. Some automatically ship from a selection of off-price merchandise—guaranteeing the vendor a small monthly stream of orders.

Terms vary greatly. Some vendors allow unsold merchandise to be returned within a short period of time; some allow no returns of promotional or off-price merchandise.

104.
Contest for Best Displays

Sponsor an annual contest for the retailer who creates the best display of your merchandise. To increase the number of winners, increase the number of categories, such as: best window display, best spot display, and best use of fixturing. The display must include the props or signage that you provide, and entries with pictures must be electronically submitted.

105.
Retailers and Vendors that Play Together, Stay Together

Here's a twist on the retail retreat that is also a mini-trade show or educational event—the cruise that puts retail winners together with the vendor's key personnel. This travel incentive for retailers has no agenda other than having a good time and being together with retailers from other parts of the country that sell your merchandise. The friendships that form around these common ties can produce indirect benefits for the vendor.

106.
Create Your Own Credit Card

More and more vendors are accepting payments from their retailers with credit cards. This is a win/win situation, because the retailer can choose to stretch out the payments without hassle (other than monthly interest) and the vendor gets out of the credit business. Sometimes the manufacturer joins forces with a credit card vendor to create its own credit card. This increases the credit limit for the retailers, who are unlikely to put personal purchases on their business cards. The other obvious benefit is having retailers walking around with your credit card in their wallets.

107.
Chases' Calendar of Events

Any vendor can develop a special occasion for its retailers and have it recognized as an international event by Chases' Calendar of Events. Chases' is also an unlimited source of existing promotional themes and events to piggyback. The best part is that there is no cost to you for having your event recognized.

108.
Make Your Catalog a Selling Tool

When you develop your catalog to show your retailers, prepare one as a tool for your retailers to share with their customers. Make sure the photos are taken to appeal to consumers, and the copy is written to resemble a print advertisement. Omit prices, of course.

ROUND UP
THE RETAILERS—
GROUP PURCHASING

ROUND UP THE RETAILERS— GROUP PURCHASING

Introduction

Vendors have a hidden asset that is seldom noticed and rarely taken advantage of: their database of customers. These customers not only purchase your merchandise but also like what you do or produce. These buyers or retailers all have similar wants, needs, and expenses. Your opportunity rests in that you know all of them, but they seldom know each other. This creates opportunities for you.

109.
What's It All About and How Can I Get Involved?

One of your hidden assets is your database of accounts, all of whom purchase similar services. All retailers buy packaging, fixtures, and display props. If you become the conduit for bringing your retailers together for volume purchases and discounts, the suppliers of these products will even pay you for the opportunity to market to your customers.

The key is to be selective and endorse only the products that you believe in and are good for your retailers. This is not the time to get greedy.

110.
Group Purchase of Web Designing Services

Group purchasing usually indicates reduced prices, but it can also make available expertise within an industry. Many retailers have trouble locating a web designer who understands the retail business. As a manufacturer, you can contract for a package with a web design firm that specializes in retailing. In addition to the volume cost benefit for your retailers, they will be dealing with someone who knows their needs.

111.
Group Buying in National and Regional Magazines

A concept that is very popular in the bridal industry can easily be adapted for other industries. As a vendor, you buy national ads and sell listings to the retailers that carry your product. Publications today can change the listings in an ad by geographical region so that a store in Texas is not listed in the New England edition.

The benefit to you is a very profitable business transaction, because the listings you sell to the retailers more than cover your costs of buying the ads. In addition, the participating retailers purchase the featured merchandise. These ads pull so well that retailers are willing to compromise on the selection of merchandise you offer through this program.

The proof of the group buying concept is *Bride's Magazine*, the largest consumer magazine in the world. Even small stores can afford the national exposure because they share the cost of an ad. It's truly a win/win/win proposition for all:

➤ the retailer, who creates a more powerful image;

➤ the consumer, who can turn a magazine into a buying resource;

➤ you, because participating retailers purchase your products;

➤ the magazine, which substantially increases its level of advertisers—for example, the January 2003 issue has pages in excess of 1,000.

Group buying works!

112.
The Printing Opportunity

Printing is one of those functions in which quantity has a substantial impact on price. That's why any group purchasing or affiliate program that you initiate with printers will become mutually profitable for you and your retailers. Some of the more popular items for group printing are signage, postcards, receipt books, service forms, purchase orders, and—in some cases—direct mail pieces.

If the Olympics can have an official printer, you can have one as well.

113.
Offer a Printed Catalog for Retailers to Buy

This concept has been around for years. Retailers buy catalogs from a buying group or a manufacturer to send to their customers. Although each retailer pays for the catalogs it buys, the cost is divided among so many retailers that the savings are substantial. The only additional printing required is putting the individual store's contact information on the front and back of their catalogs. But this should not cost you any money. And to save you the time of putting all the details together, there are companies that will produce the entire catalog for you.

114.
The Thank You Note

Upscale high-ticket retailers like to show appreciation to their customers with thank you notes. A service you can offer is the strategic alliance you form with a printer to make this gesture more cost-effective for the retailer. Offer your retailers several designs and allow them to buy these cards through you. It doesn't cost you any money and is a nice value-added service that shows you care about the retailer's business success.

115.
The Birthday Card

The birthday card is the #1 direct mail piece any retailer can use to create a lasting relationship with its own customers and diminish the typical leakage of customers. This service works the same as the Thank You Note (above)—but, as an added benefit to retailers and to you, the manufacturer encloses a gift with the birthday card: some type of coupon or special offer, with a time restriction, of course.

You've seen the birthday card and coupon idea used by restaurants. The coupon usually offers a free birthday meal or dessert, good only for seven days at the time of the birthday.

116.
Make a Hot Item Hotter in Full Color

Direct mail is still the #1 vehicle for retail advertising today, but retailers too often run out of ideas and material to send their customers. Nothing is more enticing than a photo of a hot item from the manufacturer. Full-color postcards with the store's logo printed on the card can be sold to the retailer at a nominal price, or charged against the co-op advertising account—or just given to the retailer.

117.
Create Local Advertising Groups

If you have several retailers located in the same trade area, assist them in creating group ads to increase their advertising power. Obviously, these stores should not directly compete with one another. They might be located in different towns but all carry a specific line.

In the Greater Boston area, six jewelry stores carrying the same designer line formed a group—sponsored and promoted by the vendor—who purchased a full-color ad in the *Boston Globe*. Although each individual store would have had difficulty justifying that type of advertising cost, with six businesses sharing the expense, this full-color ad became extremely cost-efficient. The vendor's time to coordinate the group effort was time well spent.

118.

Supplying Store Fixtures

To create a brand presence in stores and help the retailers display your merchandise, offer incentives for free racks and fixtures. Incentives can be earned in numerous ways:

➤ From the retailer's purchase of a minimum amount

➤ From co-op dollars

➤ From a reduced price on a group buy.

These fixtures generally have your company name on them. Even more important is for you to make these fixtures so distinctive that they are recognizable as yours even without your company name on it.

One of the leaders in marketing via distinctive store fixture is the accessory company, Brighton. Its logo and racks have the same look and feel, making them unique and extremely recognizable.

IT'S SHOW TIME!—
TRADE SHOWS

It's Show Time!—
Trade Shows

Introduction

A major portion of a vendor's revenue and a retailer's spending occurs during a multi-day conclave we refer to as the trade show. As much as technology has tried to eliminate the live trade show, it is here to stay because it's about more than just buying merchandise. It's about making face-to-face contact with the people you do business with. It's a time to network with colleagues and contemporaries, and it is a time to learn from the experts and those in the trenches.

Every second spent at a trade show counts. What follows are tips from two retailers who have attended over 1,000 trade shows in every industry in every corner of the United States. We share what your retailers would like to see every vendor do.

Section A.
Before and After the Show

We've all seen the exhibitors who come rushing into the exhibit hall at the last minute. They check to see if the show producers have brought the boxes just shipped overnight by FedEx, to verify that a couple of tables and chairs are available in the space, to identify who is exhibiting near them, and to locate the restrooms and food vendors. Then they proceed to unload their samples, hopeful that someone at the factory remembered to include order forms and maybe a sample of the new item the sales manager has been telling them about.

We've also seen the exhibitors who have taken the time to make the most of the trade show. Here are some of <u>their</u> ideas.

119.
Pre-Show Mailings

Send a mailing to your retailers clearly explaining the reasons why they should visit your booth. It must be more than just the standard, "We have a hot line." If you are offering show incentives, tell your retailers what they are, and make sure these are real incentives—not "make believe" bargains that will be available after the show. If you are introducing a new product, explain why it belongs in the retailer's store and what customer profile the product was designed for.

120.
The Pre-Show Call

This can be the "make or break" point of the exhibitor's trade show experience. The most obvious reason for calling retailers before a show is as a reminder to avoid the "out of sight, out of mind" syndrome. You do not want retailers to forget about you when they arrive at the show. Ask any retailer and you'll hear that he or she has simply forgotten to visit a specific vendor.

The pre-show call is also an opportunity to entice the buyer by reinforcing the show specials described in your mailing. This is the time to make appointments for showing product lines and writing orders.

121.
Trade Show Training—It Shows!

As good as you might think you are, the best of us needs a refresher course from a trade show training professional. Certain companies specialize in this type of training, such as The Tradeshow Coach. These companies can assist you with trade show sales techniques as well as the etiquette needed to deal with the number of "tire kickers" who attend trade shows.

122.
Design Your Exhibit Floor Plan

Plan your traffic flow. Where will your displays be set up? Where will your tables go? How will people enter and exit? Make it easy for someone to get into your booth, feel comfortable enough to stay there, write an order without feeling that someone is looking over their shoulder, and exit without difficulty. Don't settle for putting merchandise in the back with a table and two chairs in the front of the display. Make the booth look inviting.

123.
Get the Bugs Out

It's extremely annoying for a buyer to shop a booth where the salespeople are unfamiliar and uncomfortable with the setup. Practice at your place. Create a mock booth and live scenarios. If you have a sales team working at different trade shows, standardize your booth with a schematic layout.

124.
Call in the Pros

Hire a professional to decorate your booth. It makes a difference. Customers want different and exciting, so make your booth look that way. It's show biz.

125.
Be Cautious in Hiring Outside Sales Help

If you must use temporary help to staff your booth, spend the time and money to educate these people about your merchandise, your company, its policies, and its mission. Just as important, teach outside sales help the proper responses for when they don't know the answer to a question. Part of the reason retailers attend shows is to see the folks who have extensive knowledge of the products. They understand that it's not always possible for the most knowledgeable person to be available when they drop by, but they do expect more than a "pretty face."

126.
After the Order, I Still Love You

Develop a method for following up with each retailer who has placed an order at the show. It can be as simple as a phone call, e-mail, or thank you note. Be sure to include an acknowledgment of what was ordered, and ask how sales are going.

127.
Send a Thank You Note

Send all retailers a note of thanks for stopping by your exhibit even if they did not buy anything. The note might be just enough to predispose the retailer to see that you get the order next time.

128.
Move into the Right Neighborhood

Always ask the show producers to situate you near complementary vendors. Being close to your competitors is far better than being placed in an aisle with merchandise that your buyers would never purchase. Positioning is seldom easy to accomplish, but never stop trying. Be a squeaky wheel if you want to get noticed at a show.

129.
Location, Location, Location

Never stop asking the show's producer what the requirements are for situating your booth in certain locations. The favorite spots almost always include:

➤ the ends of aisles

➤ the first booth seen when people enter the exhibition area

➤ next to food service areas.

130.
Wear the Pre-show Pin

In your pre-show mailings to your retailers, send a lapel pin or button that is colorful, easily distinguished, and bears a logo or phrase relating to your company. Invite your retailers to wear the pin during the show, come to your exhibit, and receive a gift. Make sure the gift you are giving is one that makes it worth the retailer's time.

Section B.
The Look of the Booth

Introduction

You are walking past a group of stores in a mall. You stop at the entrance to each store to take a look. For various reasons, you end up spending considerable time looking more closely at only a few and wandering into the store to look at what's inside. You pass by the majority of shops quickly, giving these only a hasty glance and not venturing inside.

The reason you are discriminating is obvious; only a few shops get your attention. You are curious and want to see more. With these stores the chances of your making a purchase are great. With the other stores the chance that you will spend any money is nil.

Exhibits at a trade show are a lot like storefronts in a mall. What follows are ideas from the exhibitors who have had the most success.

131.
Display Merchandise as in the Store

Too often, manufacturers create beautiful displays that have no connection with the way retailers actually merchandise the product in their stores. Be sure to create displays that are easily adaptable to a store setting, and offer documentation and/or photographs so retailers can duplicate the displays themselves.

132.
Use the Booth Display as a Store Prototype

Develop fixtures, signs, and display techniques that your retailers can purchase through you. Or provide copies of the blueprints for building purposes. Your goal is to create the optimum fixture/display presentation to maximize sell-through of your products and to offer solutions or ideas for the retailer.

133.

Use the Height of Your Booth

Consider expanding your display above the traditional 8-foot height of the pipe and drape. Many shows do not allow it, but just as many have no rules about it. One good use for the height is to hang balloons or streamers.

134.

Make the Rear of Your Exhibit a Magnet

Have some attraction at a higher elevation at the rear of your exhibit to draw the retailer into the booth. It should be an eye-catching item—large and colorful—such as a product, a logo, or a creative sign.

135.
Booth Identification Signage

Make your signs visible from every possible angle so a retailer can quickly know where you are. Doing so is simple, but the majority of trade show exhibitors ignore this obvious advantage. They settle instead for the identification signage provided by the exhibit hall and fail to do anything that reaches beyond the extremities of their booth.

Consider floor signage. Angled signs that stand 2 feet to 4 feet in height take advantage of the fact that people walking by a booth are not looking up. Lacking signage at this height is an opportunity lost. Bring all your own identifying signs and include them within your display.

136.
Signage is Good Service

Use lots of signs within your exhibit to identify you and your product and to provide information about your product. Retailers who shop trade shows regard signage as a form of good service—the same way the consumer regards the signage in a store.

137.
How Low Can You Go?

Display merchandise at least 30 inches off the floor. Merchandise below this level, if seen at all, requires visitors to bend over—and that takes up more space in your booth.

138.
The Electronic Message Board

High-tech solutions exist for almost everything today, and the electronic message board has certainly come of age. It is easier to program and to change messages than with a printed sign. The key to an effective electronic message board is to not only inform but also cause the visitor to interact with the booth. On the sign, say who you are and what you sell.

Boring signs do not sell. So have the sign ask a question. For example:

➤ Do you need ____?

➤ Would you like ____?

➤ When was the last time ____?

➤ Did you pay too much?

➤ Have you shopped everybody?

The goal is to create a moment of interaction. Facts tell, but stories sell!

139.
Keep Your Booth Clean and Professional

The way your booth looks tells something about you and your company. Don't expect to attract quality retailers if you don't project an image of the quality resource. If you are using a rep firm, make sure they adhere to the same standards, because it will hurt your image if they don't.

140.
Eliminate the Distractions

Telephones, newspapers, and magazines for personal use in your booth turn off visitors. They cause clutter, making the vendor appear unprofessional—a company that retailers don't want to do business with.

141.
Branding Means Consistency and Distinctiveness

Everyone understands the power of brand. Whatever the visitors to your booth experience also has branding power. Be distinctive and be consistent—with everything you do, from the materials you hand out to the refreshments you serve. If you give away candy or cookies, make them distinctive enough that your visitors will talk about them. One vendor has fortune cookies specially made for every show.

Review every second a retailer will experience at your booth, from the first hello to the last good-bye—including the ability to touch the merchandise. The goal is to have the retailer not only buy but also say, "[Your Company Name] was a great booth."

142.
Is the Fixture a Friend or Foe?

Be careful not to block pathways with fixtures. Not only do such displays restrict passage, but the displays also run the risk of becoming dismantled by the constant bumping and jarring. They may be interesting, but don't they defeat the purpose of having the booth?

143.
Open Wide

Your exhibit should be arranged like a funnel, with the largest opening at the aisle or entrance to the booth. The purpose of a wide entrance is to create an inviting feeling while being less intimidating— just as a grocery store has a lobby area as you enter.

Paco Underhill's book *Why We Buy* presents extensive research about the "butt-brush factor." This means that if people feel they are brushing against other people to move around, they opt not to enter the space.

144.
Down in Front

Arrange the merchandise in your exhibit so it cascades from front to rear, with the tallest merchandise in the back and the shortest in front. In this way, visitors are able see into your whole exhibit when they are deciding whether to stop.

145.
Don't Create Obstacles

Avoid using a table at the front of the booth as your desk. Doing so looks unprofessional and demonstrates a lack of effort to create an inviting environment. It also blocks the path to the merchandise. Exhibit-goers seldom stop at booths that create obstacles—or if they stop, they don't stay and interact with the merchandise. Retailers need an opportunity to look at the merchandise before they make the mental commitment to sit down and write an order.

146.
Carpet Accents

Use a different color carpet from other exhibitors. You can also add different designs with custom cuts of carpet.

147.
Use Laptops Effectively

Unless you are using a laptop computer to create orders, show catalogs of your product offering, or run a pre-programmed presentation, don't have a laptop in your booth.

148.
Never Underestimate the Power of Lighting

The more light you can add to your exhibit, the more retailers you will attract. Lighting sells. There is no excuse for not having the proper spotlights and lighting treatments. The size of the equipment is so small and the costs are reasonable enough that even the smallest of reps can properly light an exhibit. The only word of caution is to learn what restrictions the exhibit hall has on types of lights and amount of foot-candles.

149.
Special Lighting Treatments

Increase your opportunity to catch the buyer's eye by using image-projecting light fixtures positioned to display your logo or message on the ceiling, walls, or floors of the exhibit hall.

150.
Make the Action Things Active

If your exhibit contains products, displays, or props that move or must be turned on, be sure they work—such as lamps, radios, water fountains, remote controls, computers, and presentations. Test each one daily.

151.
Displaying Your Ads

Creative, provocative, image-building, and even controversial advertisements make great posters. And great posters make great trade show displays. They:

➤ reinforce the ad

➤ create consistency

➤ align the booth with the product, and

➤ show the merchandise in the way it was intended to be shown.

They also make a relatively simple display prop.

. . . .

Some advertisements that make great posters have even become cult or pop classics, such as the Calvin Klein underwear ads that have become popular posters, especially in college dormitories worldwide. Yours might become a collector's item, too.

. . . .

152.
The Show Must Go On–Continuous DVD

Running a video at your booth isn't a new idea, but what you choose to run can differentiate you from others. Many vendors run videos of their product line—which is okay—but showing retailers how the product can be displayed or merchandised in the store is more practical and helpful. And showing sample ads or the ways the vendor would like the product promoted can sometimes be a retailer's deciding factor in whether to order the merchandise.

153.
Create a Dress Code

A vendor must look professional. Clothes can be a turn-off or a turn-on. That's why companies are increasingly going for logo-imprinted shirts or tops. The only problem is that vendors are starting to look alike with their denim shirts. But you know the answer: <u>do something different.</u>

154.
Dress in a Costume

If you really want to attract attention, add a creative flair to how your booth personnel dress. Depending on your product, a costume can be as simple as wearing white coats to look like doctors or a cap and gown to look like a professor. Obviously you can go to much greater extremes—but even a tuxedo can go a long way to setting a mood.

155.
Create a Theme Just for Your Booth

Trade shows have themes, so why can't you? Decorate your booth with a specific theme, wear related costumes, and watch the excitement and the word-of-mouth advertising build.

156.
Tie into the Trade Show Theme

If the trade show has a theme, use that theme in your booth in as many ways as possible—display, signage, decorations, snacks—even the attire of your booth's personnel. If it doesn't impress your buyers, it will certainly impress the show organizers who came up with the theme. They are the ones who might be referring attendees to take a look at your booth, and they may be the ones to give you a better booth placement at a future show.

One vendor we've seen has built a reputation by consistently tying into the theme of the trade show, making his booth a "must see" for every buyer. The interpretation of the show theme and its implementation makes this booth a true show-stopper.

If you are selling skateboards, your booth has to look young, hip, bright, and—of course—extreme. You want the music loud and the personnel urban chic.

Whatever your product, make sure its <u>setting</u> is in alignment with your buyer's vision, image, product, and—most important—expectations.

It's showtime!

Section C.
The Moment of Contact—
Interaction at the Booth

Introduction

"Step right up. Come right on in. Everyone gather 'round. The show is about to start." Expressions like these have worked, and continue to work for the carnival barker. Crowds do gather, and people give their money to see what the excitement is.

However, most show producers won't let you hire a carnival barker to stand in front of your booth. And if your sales reps attempt this, buyers go out of their way to avoid them. (There will also be that visit from the show producer telling you to stop "hawking people in the aisles.")

There must be a way to get some attention at your exhibit. And here are our 21st-century ideas for ways to get folks to "come right on in."

157.
Make it Fun and They Will Come

We live in an entertainment-based society. The larger vendors build their booths the same way that a Broadway producer builds a set. The excitement can be captured for much less money, however, with the use of fun, playful, and creative signage posted throughout the booth. Three guidelines for good signage are:

➤ Interesting but readable fonts

➤ Color

➤ Creative copy

Make it look like fun but remember—content is king. The electronic message board can be a great tool to implement a fun or playful strategy. Use it to flash fun quotes, or a playful riddle (with answers to follow). You can keep buyers at your booth for a longer time as they wait for the answers to appear.

158.
Honor Your Appointment Times

One of the worst things reps do is to make appointments and not honor the time commitment with the buyer. Be aware that buyers will hesitate to make appointments with your reps for future shows if they are forced to wait.

159.
No Loitering Here

We are fully aware that sales reps at a trade show are not busy every moment, and that they occasionally socialize with other reps. Most visitors understand that, so two reps talking together may be acceptable. However, one of the most intimidating experiences for a buyer is to encounter a group of three or more sales reps. The buyer feels like an intruder, an uninvited guest—not part of the clique. So be sure your reps remain aware that a trade show is about making the buyer feel comfortable.

160.
Never Drop One Customer for Another

When working with a smaller account at your booth, as tempting it may be to drop them while you focus on a bigger account, don't do it. It always comes back to haunt you. Besides, the bigger account won't respect you for it either.

161.
Book Signing at Your Booth

Find out who is speaking at your trade show and invite him or her to your booth for a 30-minute book signing. Many times you can get the speaker/ expert to stay at your booth for a little while to meet your customers. If you invite a different speaker every day, your booth will become the place where things are happening.

162.
Hold a Mini-Seminar at the Booth

Invite experts to do presentations on topics ranging from product presentation or display to advertising. Set up chairs in your booth to limit attendance—not only because you don't have much room, but also because it will make retailers want to come back for the next event.

163.
Sense Management—Sight

There are five senses. In setting up your booth, try to appeal to all five, starting with the most obvious, sight.

Allow your customers to view what you are selling. Don't clutter your booth with obstacles or crowded merchandise. Concentrate on the excitement of the merchandise, not on the fixture or the wall. Make sure you differentiate the look of your booth. Focus the buyer's eye on your exhibit by consciously blocking the view of competing exhibits with signage, fixturing, props, or walls.

164.
Sound Sense

Have background music playing, not too loud to affect the neighboring exhibits but enough to help put your customer in the type of mood you want to create. Many companies that sell mood music are willing to supply the music for your booth in return for a promotional mention at your booth.

165.
The Right Touch

Allow your visitors to touch the merchandise. Many people need to feel the goods in order to buy. Though touching is more important in some areas of retail than in others, if this is the dominant sense for buyers visiting your exhibit, you must be able to accommodate their needs.

166.
Trade Show Massage Therapy

Many trade shows have a massage therapist for hire in the common areas of the exhibit hall. A welcome variation is to have a massage therapist at your booth for a couple of hours late in the day. These can be neck and shoulder massages that take up no more booth space than the chair the visitor sits in. Buyers will come and stay at your booth longer than they ever intended. You could also offer a "free massage with each order written."

167.

A Sense of Smell

This is the most overlooked but frequently the most important of the five senses. It's time to be blunt here. No one wants to stay at a booth where the salesperson smells from bad breath, cigarette smoke, body odor, or strong perfume or cologne. Sometimes it's the merchandise that has a smell, either from manufacturing or from being shipped from a distant land. Whatever it is, bad smells don't sell!

On the other hand, there are positive smells, but you have to be careful, because what is positive to one person can repel another. Many people love the smell of vanilla, lilac, or pumpkin; however, we do not recommend their use at a trade show because just as many people can be turned off by them. And some people are allergic to perfume and scented room deodorizers.

The safest scent is something that will create a fresh, clean, or outdoor feeling. Check out the new electric candle warmers that allow you to extract the scent of a candle without lighting it. And, depending on the refreshments you plan to serve, the smell of fresh-baked cookies or popcorn can draw people to your booth.

130

168.
In Good Taste

Tickling the taste buds offers many possibilities, from serving food at the booth to offering hard candy or M&Ms. Although it's not necessary, it is a nice touch that will reinforce your brand. Customers stay when something to eat is available. Exhibitors are known to differentiate themselves by the food they offer— sometimes as simple as homemade chocolate chip cookies baked just for the show, year after year. Continuity like this helps to build the brand.

The food offered should be in alignment with the level of quality of the merchandise. If you are selling high quality merchandise, reflect that quality in your giveaways.

One exhibitor placed an old-fashioned Coke machine in the booth. Before putting the Cokes in the cooler, he put a sticker on each bottle identifying the company, his name, and the booth location.

169.
Giveaways

Give something away to retailers that they can put on their clothing while at the show. Make sure the product is unique. At a college book show, we once saw a vendor giving out felt stickers of favorite college teams. Avoid T-shirts or other promotional items that other people cannot see <u>during</u> the show. The idea is to make other attendees head for your booth to get <u>theirs</u>.

170.
The Best Giveaway

The shopping bag as a giveaway is an old trick, but it works best with this new twist. Instead of having only the vendor's name on the bag, add an introductory line such as: "I just saw the new line at Booth #___." Put some sell into it.

The only word of caution is that if you are going to be preprinting bags with the booth number on it, make sure you have the correct number and that you don't order too many, because you cannot carry them over to another show.

Canvas bags are great but expensive. A good high-quality plastic or paper shopping bag can be just as effective. But make it big. Remember—it's the biggest and heaviest bag that all of the other bags are put into.

171.
Make Trade Show Specials <u>Special</u>

Offer a special that is good only at the show. Do not allow this offer to apply after the show or you will lose credibility and diminish the importance of attending the show. Some vendors offer additional savings for the first day of the show, or for the first hour of the show. Their purpose is to create activity during slower times and to build momentum.

172.
The Surprise Special

Hold special promotional offerings in your booth during the trade show. Consider having different unannounced specials in your booth at different times of the day to induce return visits. Be careful how you construct the promotion so you anticipate anything that might make the buyer reluctant to leave an order. You might give a free gift with orders placed before 10 a.m., for example. Or—to encourage reorders at the same time a regular order is placed—you might offer a larger discount for doubling the quantity ordered of any style or model.

173.
Card Collection Incentives

Marketing people like to say that we are in the name collection business, and that the more prospects we have, the greater the opportunity to sell. That's why many trade-show booths offer daily giveaways.

➤ The most common giveaway method invites passersby to drop their business cards into a bowl from which a daily winner is drawn.

➤ Riddles, trivia questions, or a question-of-the-day are announced, inviting visitors to write their answers on the back of their business cards for a later drawing.

➤ Some vendors make donations to a charity in the name of the retailer whose business card is drawn from the collection of cards.

➤ One of the more popular giveaways we observed was the coupon for free pizza offered for every business card received.

Whatever your technique, the goal is to collect business cards that eventually turn into business.

134

174.
Interactive Contests– Bring 'Em Back Alive

Have a blackboard or a white board that announces the winners of each contest. By offering a daily drawing and posting the winners' names, you draw extra traffic to your booth. The traffic makes your booth look busy, and retailers like to do business with busy companies. Many retailers who shop a show make a point of shopping only the busy booths.

175.
Instant Answers

Maintain on-line access to your office so you can assist buyers with anything while they are at your booth. This includes accounting, shipping, and production.

176.

Leaving Paper Incentives

The expression "leaving paper" refers to a buyer's placing an order for merchandise with the sales rep at the time of the presentation. Getting buyers to do this is becoming more difficult, however, so the incentive must be greater than ever before. Some vendors offer a 2 or 3 percent discount on an entire order if placed at the time of the presentation. Others offer a 5 percent discount if placed then but a 3 percent discount if placed before the show ends.

One of the biggest obstacles to leaving paper is the retailers not knowing exactly how much money is being spent. Overcome this obstacle with technology; use a laptop and computerized ordering techniques to complete the order when it is placed. The same technology also lets the vendor check the account's credit limit. Work with the retailer to make it a solid order.

177.
Create a Retail Advisory Panel

Don't be afraid to ask your retailers for their opinions. Their vast knowledge about the way to sell merchandise represents an untapped resource of expertise for you. And they will be flattered when asked to serve on your panel.

Recruit 6 to 10 panel members, each of whom demonstrates these qualifications:

➤ is a trade show regular

➤ runs a good business

➤ is respected within the industry

➤ is progressive

➤ offers a different point of view.

Plan a breakfast for your advisory panel members held once during an annual show and lasting no more than 75 minutes. The purpose is to pick their brains and get them to share ideas on topics ranging from their show experience to business trends to ways you can improve your business. When ideas are shared in a group, people's combined energy inspires greater insight. You not only benefit from this powerhouse of ideas but also cement relationships. (Also see Tip #23.)

178.
Know the Score—Help Buyers Track What They Spend

Retailers often place numerous orders at a trade show, only to return to their stores and discover that they spent more than they'd planned. Help them overcome this problem by creating a form and printing it on a card, which retailers can use to record their own running total of the buying dollars they spend. Each line of information should include vendor name, purchase order number, ship date, terms, and order total. The back of the card can be imprinted with information about your company—a handy record that also leaves a reminder of your business in the buyer's pocket.

179.
The Suggestion Process

Trade show attendees offer an even broader pool of untapped ideas than an advisory group, especially if you offer an incentive, such as a key chain, pen, or shopping bag—with your logo on it, of course. Have a comment card that asks retailers for their comments, ideas, and suggestions for how you can improve your business. Ask, for example, "What one thing could we do to make it easier for you to do business with us at the show?"

180.
Every Opinion Counts

Less formal than the advisory group or the comment card is to simply ask the retailers who visit your booth what they think of the booth and how you could improve it. Everyone loves a person who is humble enough to ask other people's opinions.

181.
The Best Suggestion

By now you realize we love competitions. We live in a very competitive society. There is no better way to bond with retailers than to have them win competitions and see their winning ideas put into practice. Give retailers an engraved plaque that they can hang in their stores. Call it a "Creativity Award for Contributions to the Success of [Your Company Name]." Plaques are not expensive, and they can go a long way toward building customer relations. And when the retailer hangs up the plaque, people will talk about your company.

182.
The Daily Wrap—
Summarizing and Debriefing

If all your sales reps are asking every customer for opinions, have a brief wrap-up meeting each day to determine the top 10 suggestions of the day.

The incentive for the sales reps is knowing that they are working for a company that is constantly trying to improve itself.

183.
Do You See What I See?
Shopping the Competition.

Don't sneak around trying not to look like a spy. Openly shop your competition and invite them to shop you. It's good business for both of you. You don't fight a war without knowing "the enemy."

184.
It's Party Time—
The After-Show Soirée

Retailers love being invited to cocktail parties. It makes them feel important. Cocktail parties should last no longer than two hours and should take place immediately upon the ending of the show day. It's a nice touch and creates some wonderful networking time.

185.
Come On Over To Our Place

Ask the show producer if you can host an after-hours cocktail reception in your booth for your accounts. Most likely you will be required to pay for security for the rest of the show floor. But your booth will get added exposure.

186.
The Hospitality Suite

Consider booking a hotel suite close to the trade show for hosting cocktail parties for key accounts and for meetings.

187.
The Networking Opportunity

Retailers don't always get the opportunity to know or socialize with other retailers. This creates an opportunity for the vendor because the vendor knows the retailers. Plan to hold a networking dinner or breakfast, and ask someone—such as one of the speakers at the trade show—to help facilitate the networking process for a modest compensation. The networking process can have retailers offer opinions in response to a question asked of the whole group. Or invite people to ask a question of the group.

188.

Power Networking Concept

If you really want your networking event to be a winner, consider a technique called Power Networking. Line up two rows of chairs facing each other about 4 feet apart. Instruct participants to take a seat across from someone they do not know. They have 5 minutes to tell the person opposite them who they are, what they do, something interesting about themselves, and what they want to accomplish at the show. The facilitator announces when 5 minutes are up, and the focus switches to the person opposite.

At the end of the second 5 minutes, the facilitator has the group change seats so everyone is again facing someone they do not know. The process can continue for up to four complete rounds. Always leave time at the end so that the brief connections can be expanded.

189.

Sponsor a Trade Show Speaker

Trade shows are starting to defray their own costs for professional speakers by having vendors sponsor them. There are many good reasons for your company to be a sponsor.

a) Your company name is listed every place the speaker's name is listed, including all pre-show mailings, all signage, and all trade show publications.

b) You have the opportunity to hand out brochures about your product together with the speaker's handouts and to say a few words before the speaker starts.

c) The speaker always thanks and recognizes the vendor's commitment to the education of their industry.

d) The public relations benefits and positioning of your company are almost priceless, especially if sponsorship is done on a consistent basis.

Once you start to sponsor such an event, other vendors will jump on the bandwagon, so be the first—and anticipate a long-term commitment.

190.
Cause Marketing

We all want to do business with companies that care and are willing to give back. Have your company become the leader in your industry by getting involved and helping someone who needs help. Sponsor a charity event on one night of the trade show. It can be a cocktail party, a networking dinner, or even a workshop for which you charge—with the proceeds going to your favorite charity. Besides being the right thing to do, it will prove that the more you give, the more you get back.

191.
The Power of the Survey

Survey the retailers who stop by your booth about a specific topic. Polling is powerful because respondents appreciate knowing the results and respect the validity of the source: other retailers like themselves. Questions can be very simple, such as "Is your business stronger or weaker than last year?" Surveys work because they set you apart from your competition by demonstrating that you care about the retailer's business. A poll is also a great way to capture names. And it's another way to get retailers talking about you and returning to your booth, especially if you post the results daily during the show.

192.
Kids are Customers Too!

Have something in your booth for the children— coloring books and crayons for younger ones, a video game for the older kids.

193.
Give 'Em a Second Chance— Interactively

After the show, send a report to all the buyers who visited your booth and identify the 5 or 10 bestselling items ordered during the show. Take an "I thought you'd want to know" approach. If they purchased those styles or models, congratulate them. If they didn't, include a fax-back order sheet to place an order with these styles. Enclose a note telling them that this is a second chance to include these hot items in their order.

194.
The Guest Appearance

Arrange for one of your product designers to be at your booth to visit with retailers. The key is to announce the time(s) that he or she will be available, promoting the event through postcards, press releases, your newsletter, and the show's daily bulletin board.

You might even set up a digital camera and printer so retailers can have their pictures taken with the designer and get them autographed.

195.
Make It a Kodak moment

Take a digital photo together with each of your customers and send it to them a week or so after the trade show. Digital cameras today allow you to take lots of pictures with very little cost. What could be of greater interest than getting a photo of oneself? And the sales rep in the photo standing next to the retailer is also a great reminder of your company, especially with your booth's signage in the background.

196.
Can I Take a Picture?

It is common at trade shows for visiting retailers to ask to take pictures of your booth's displays and merchandise. Have a camera available for the use of those customers. Granted, other vendors are doing the same thing, but you can improve your sales by using a digital camera, computer, and printer so you can hand the retailer pictures of the products they buy and of your displays.

197.
Take a Walk and Tap a Hidden Asset

Accompany your better accounts on a walk through the show and let them point out to you what they are buying. Offer to buy them a soda or cup of coffee. Listening to what they have to say demonstrates that you are interested in their business and the success of their store. You also gain a better perspective on their thinking.

BUYING—
WHERE THE RUBBER
MEETS THE ROAD

BUYING—
WHERE THE RUBBER
MEETS THE ROAD

Introduction

P utting pen to paper to write the order is the actual moment when the retailer begins to spend money. If only it were that easy—for both parties—to make a simple decision about color, quantity, size, and delivery date. Since that is not the case, the vendor has many ways for assisting a retailer in writing not only the first order, but many orders for years to come.

Here are some of the best ideas we can share with you. These are collected from our individual experiences as retailers, as well as from the many retailers who continually share their own ideas with each of us.

198.
Buying Incentives

A nice way of thanking a retailer for placing an order is to reward each with a premium—such as a book on retailing. Some good ones are:

➤ *Raving Fans*

➤ *The Experience Economy*

➤ *Why We Buy*

➤ *Predatory Marketing*

➤ *Marketing Warfare*

➤ *Retail Business Kit for Dummies*

➤ *EZ Cashflow*

➤ *The E-Myth.*

199.
Send Reminders of Orders

Develop a system to remind retailers that it's time to buy. Include each retailer's previous year's order summary, and even an ad featuring a current lead product. Use any communication method you prefer—mail, e-mail, fax, postcard.

200.
Scale Your Co-op Program

Reward the loyal retailers who advertise consistently by giving them an increase in the co-op fund percentage. This means that the retailer who runs 20 ads per year gets a larger incentive than the retailer who advertises 3 times a year.

201.
Making Reorders Easy

Simplify the buying process on reordered items by sending your retailers an on-hand inventory form. Include style numbers, sizes, colors, and any other information necessary for ordering. The form allows retailers to fill in their own on-hand inventory so they are able to place an intelligent reorder. Send inventory forms to existing accounts, and offer an incentive if they bring their completed forms to an upcoming trade show.

202.
I Like Your Style– Respect Different Buying Styles

People like different ways of buying and selling. Some retailers like to review the entire line, then go back to make purchases. Others like to write as they go through the line. Some buyers like to have the salesperson make recommendations as to what is hot and what is not.

Explain to each retailer how you like to sell and let each retailer explain the style in which she or he likes to buy. Whatever style is preferred, establish it at the outset.

203.
Have it Your Way!

Identify how and where each retailer likes to buy. With the advent of technology, retailers have a choice of ways to purchase goods. It can be online with a PowerPoint presentation, in the store at certain hours, or at a show, with or without an appointment. Learn their preferences and work around them.

204.
Try It—You'll Like It

Whenever you recommend a specific item to a retailer, justify your recommendation with a good reason for the retailer to buy it. Be specific. Even if it is just a hunch or an educated guess, say so. The retailer would love to know.

205.
"Everybody is Buying That"

Just because everyone else is buying a particular item doesn't mean recommending it to every retailer. Sales reps have an obligation to inform their buyers of the merchandise that is a top seller, but it might not be right for every store. If anything, popularity is one reason not to buy something, because if everyone carries the same thing, the retailer can't make any extra margin. Have your reps use any of a number of other benefit statements besides one that screams "low margin item."

206.
Let's Get Personal

A sales rep's opinion can be very important to retailers because reps are educated observers who spend their lives in retail businesses. So retailers listen when your company's rep:

➤ observes that the retailer already carries Lines X, Y, and Z

➤ explains that your company's Lines A, B, and C fit well in stores carrying those other lines, and

➤ offers a personal or professional opinion about why an item or line of merchandise should be carried.

Even if retailers initially reject a proposed line, they have to respect the salesperson who persists with the retailer's best interest in mind.

207.
2/10 EOM Net 30X Means What?

Too many times the retailer doesn't understand the terms of an order and is too embarrassed to ask.

Explain the terms in a matter-of-fact way that keeps the retailer from feeling stupid.

208.
You Want it When?

One of the biggest issues for retailers is having merchandise flow into the store in a timely manner. When a retailer gives you 4 months to deliver an order and you know that 90 percent of the merchandise won't be shipped until the last 10 days of the delivery cycle, inform the retailer. Eliminate the 4-month window. Lowering the frustration level helps the retailer and makes you a more valuable resource.

209.
Tell Me About Yourself

Have your sales reps explain any idiosyncrasies the retailer will experience by placing an order with your company. Volunteer information about:

➤ Whether the manufacturer ships early.

➤ How much credit will be extended.

➤ If an extra 30 days can be taken for payment.

➤ If the merchandise comes in ready for sale or if preparation is required.

➤ Whether the contact people prefer communication by e-mail, fax, or phone.

➤ What makes the company different or strange.

157

210.
Just Charge It!

Have your sales reps tell the retailer if payment can be made with a credit card and if there is a surcharge for doing so. No one likes being billed for hidden charges or for merchandise not yet received, so always explain how the retailer might be affected by a credit transaction with your company. With credit cards earning airline bonus miles, even a small retailer who spends only $100,000 could be entitled to 4 airline tickets. This is becoming an important point.

211.
Why Charge for Extra Dating?

If a retailer becomes over-extended and requires extra dating, do not charge them "credit card" interest rates. If they need a little extra help, offer it— it will go a long way.

212.

Your Form or Mine

Whose form to use is an age-old problem. Both retailers and manufacturers like to use their own standardized order forms. Both may have conditions they like to preprint on their order forms. Make sure you come to some agreement about whose form will be used and whose policies and conditions each party to a transaction is accepting.

213.

Consignment Merchandise

Do you allow goods to go into a store and have them paid for when sold? Consignment arrangements are major selling points for many retailers in deciding to order from your company. To increase orders, consider offering certain models and styles on consignment, giving the retailer an extra edge and adding to the size of an order. Retailers often pay for the merchandise earlier anyway. But their perception of when they may pay affects the reality of the order placed.

214.
Does This Go with What I Have?

Adding a new product line can have different effects for different retailers. Sometimes adding a new line increases the sales of other lines of merchandise the retailer carries, and sometimes it takes away sales from those existing lines. Help your retailers by sharing with them related experiences from other accounts. This is where the term "consultive selling" originates.

Merchandise has to fit the store. Reps who don't ask what other lines a retailer carries are not doing their job. And reps who don't know the impact that one line can have on another when both are carried are not properly servicing their customers.

215.
Have I Got a Deal for You!

A major component of retailing is the selling of off-price and promotional merchandise in stores specializing in this. However, retailers who are loyal to your merchandise should never be left out of off-price or promotional offers. Although it can be more expensive to offer this merchandise to multiple accounts, the price should also compensate.

216.
Exclusivity Lives

In some segments of the retail industry, having the exclusive rights to a line can be very important. Consider the following questions:

➤ Can you give the retailer an exclusive right to sell certain merchandise in a specific trading area?

➤ How long will that retailer have that right?

➤ What kind of sales volume should the retailer be expected to produce?

➤ At what point does a vendor have the right to change alliance?

➤ Does exclusivity extend to the retailer's ability to sell that merchandise on-line?

217.
How Many Do I Have to Buy?

There are different types of minimums, such as total dollar volume on an order, total dollar volume in a year, units per style, and total number of styles. Minimums are here to stay and they make sense. Many retailers don't mind paying a premium or surcharge when they break the minimum rules. But if there are other ways around the minimums, help the retailer work it out.

218.
Invite Customer or Employee Reaction

If you are working with a retailer in the store, let the employees and customers offer opinions when appropriate. The more involved they are, the better it is for you, the vendor. Argue with this phenomenon and be prepared to lose the account. Use it and the retailer could buy more.

219.
Let Me Tell You a Story

Every piece of merchandise has a story:

➤ who designed it

➤ what might be unique about that person

➤ who inspired the designer

➤ where the merchandise was made

➤ what celebrity or team might be using it

➤ and so on

The more compelling the story, the better the item will sell. Customers want reasons to buy and retailers want reasons to sell. Offer those reasons and the sale happens.

220.
Know When to Say When

There comes a time when every hot item starts to cool off. Every retailer has turned a winner into a loser with the last reorder. Vendors or manufacturers must avoid this scenario by putting some type of system in place to alert retailers when an item is starting to slow.

221.
What Size Do You Take?

Help your retailers determine their own charts of best selling sizes. Often, retailers opt out of the process and let the manufacturer give them a size range based on national sales figures. Instead, help your retailers determine the best selling sizes for their store's own clientele.

222.
Survey the Retailer

Contact your retailers and ask what would assist them most in writing orders. Answers might be:

➤ the opportunity for the retailer to get out of the store

➤ a report of sales provided to the retailer by the vendor

➤ electronic ordering that is compatible with the retailer's computer system.

A company that is constantly improving is a winning company.

164

STREET SMART STUFF—THE WHY'S BEHIND THE BUYS

STREET SMART STUFF—THE WHY'S BEHIND THE BUYS

Introduction

Maybe some retailers have logical reasons for choosing which vendors to do business with. A lot more retailers have all kinds of intangible reasons for choosing their vendors. Those small reasons add up over a period of time, making one vendor more desirable than another. We asked many of the buyers we've had the opportunity to visit:

> "Have you ever chosen one vendor over another for a reason other than price, delivery, or product selection? If so, what was it that influenced your decision?"

Here is what they told us.

223.
Laughing to the Bank—The Fun Factor

We live in an entertainment-based society in which the customer has a high regard for the entertainment value of the shopping experience. Entertainment selling and a focus on fun are becoming very accepted ways of attracting and retaining customers. Retailers need ideas, information, and methods of using fun, humor, and playful behavior to make their businesses more appealing.

Gather information from retailers who are adding these elements, capture the ideas in tips books, web sites, newspaper articles, and so on, and help all your retailers adopt this type of strategy for greater profit.

. . . .

The Rain Forest Café and the Hard Rock Café sell hamburgers and T-shirts, but the entertainment value to their customers allows them to charge higher prices than McDonald's. The lesson is to make buying fun.

. . . .

. . . .

Pike's Fish Market in Seattle changed the way a commodity item was marketed by adding fun. You might have seen this concept portrayed in the runaway bestseller *Fish*.

. . . .

224.
Communicating with Your Retailer

Everyone has some preferred way in which he or she wants to be informed. Some retailers prefer a phone call; some want it in writing; some like e-mail; some prefer fax; some want announcements on the company's web site; and some even prefer face to face contact. For the vendor who wants to become each retailer's preferred vendor, the challenge is to know which method of communication is most effective for the retailer.

225.
About Time for User-friendly Order Forms

Have an easy-to-work-with order form: easy to read, easy to understand, and in a size that fits into a standard file folder. Many retailers refuse to use certain vendors' order forms because of their legal language and the one-sided, "win/lose" position that such language communicates.

Develop a contract when the account is first set up and you will not need to restate it with each order.

226.
The Customer Comes First

If the ordering is done in the store, remember: the store's customers come first. Without customers, there is no need to place any orders. The retailer understands that your sales rep's time is important, but the sales rep needs to understand that not all retailers can afford to have additional personnel cover the sales floor while they look at your product line. Knowing that the customer comes first keeps both retailer and vendor in business.

227.
Around Customers, Everyone Sells

If you have to wait for the retailer's attention, pitch in and help with a customer. No, it's not in your job description, but small efforts go a long way. You don't have to actually wait on customers—just be helpful to support the customer's good will. The line "I am just a sales rep" doesn't cut it any more.

228.

Eliminate Retailer Surprises

Preferred vendor status depends on your retailers feeling that you work for a win/win relationship. To maintain that relationship, never leave the store feeling that you fooled your customer or got the better of the relationship. Make sure there are no surprises for the retailer. Leave knowing that the transaction is a win/win.

229.

Enough is Enough

Make sure your retailers are aware of how much they are actually buying. Over-spending is another surprise that can backfire. You don't want to feel that you pulled a fast one because the retailer was unaware of the dollar total. You are much better off getting one solid order than writing one that the retailer cancels half of a week later.

230.
How Much for Me?

Retailers are aware that discounts are available and that different prices for different buying groups are usually based on quantity levels. So let the retailer know what the criteria are for qualifying for a discount, and you will strengthen your relationship with that retailer. Be open about your discount policies.

Here are some of the questions that retailers want to ask manufacturers:

➤ Are there quantity discounts?

➤ How are they earned?

➤ Are other retailers getting a better price, and if so why?

➤ Can money be saved if a retailer pays early?

➤ If the retailer takes goods COD, is there an extra discount?

➤ Do you allow anticipation?

The vendors who have been open and fair with discounts, incentives, and price reduction policies have fared much better over the years than those who choose to use let's-make-a-deal "back room" tactics.

231.
"I am Not a Crook"

Deal with honesty and integrity. As simple and as basic as this principle is, it is not practiced by all vendors. More retailers are avoiding certain manufacturers because of it. Honesty and integrity are back in vogue. Retailers have developed a short fuse when it comes to issues of honesty. They also have long memories and they tell others about their experiences.

232.
Return Policy

Your retailers don't like getting returns any more than manufacturers do. But they know that the easier they make the returns process, the more they keep customers' good will and encourage their repeat business.

Take catalog merchants, for example. Because they ship their merchandise with easy-to-use return labels, they get repeat orders. They learned that they have to make it easy for their customer to do business with them.

Retailers need to feel this same level of confidence in doing business with a vendor.

233.
Order Cancellation Policy

This is a topic no one really wants to talk about, but it needs to be addressed. No, you do not have to spend time going over your cancellation policy with each retailer. But you should clearly state your policies, distinguish between canceling all or part of an order, and specify the steps a retailer needs to take.

Here are some areas to consider covering in your policy statements:

➤ Can an order be canceled?

➤ What penalties might there be for cancellation?

➤ What if the vendor does not ship the order by the completion date?

If orders are being placed using the retailer's own order pad, the vendor should produce a statement for retailers to read about cancellations. If the manufacturer's order form is being used, the cancellation policy should be clearly stated on it in "readable" language.

234.
It's Broken—It's Not My Fault!

Damaged merchandise isn't fun for anybody, but it's a fact of life. The major concern voiced by retailers about damages is simply not knowing what the company policy is. So be sure to let your retailers know your policy in advance. State it clearly on the purchase order. If the retailer is using his or her own order pad, state the policy on a fact sheet. Post it on your web site.

Here are some of the questions that retailers like answered:

➤ Do you have to get a return authorization?

➤ What is the waiting period for an authorization label?

➤ Will you credit the return before the goods are actually returned, and will doing so cause any problems?

➤ Can the product be destroyed in the field?

➤ Can your field sales rep handle this?

235.
Return to Sender

What is the manufacturer's policy on returning merchandise? Similar to the issue of damaged merchandise, your policy on returns must be clearly stated. Retailers simply need to know their options.

Here are some concerns to address in your policy:

➤ Can a retailer return merchandise?

➤ What is the time frame for even inquiring about a return?

➤ How do you handle time-sensitive merchandise?

➤ Can slow sellers be substituted for different styles?

➤ How do you handle a government recall or manufacturer recall of a product?

236.
Discounters and Mass Merchants

No retailer can ever fault a vendor who chooses to sell the same merchandise to discounters or mass merchants. The retailers are only trying to protect the integrity of their store and their prices. They just want to know who their competition is. There is nothing worse than repressing that information. You might win the war but you will lose the account.

237.
On-line Retailers and Non-Storefront Retailers

Make your retailers aware that they might also have competition on-line. Just as the retailer has the right to put the manufacturer's merchandise on their web site, the manufacturer has the right to list all the ways that consumers can get their products. To keep the good will of your retailers, keep them informed. Let them know that e-commerce is changing the way we do business, and that business models are being recreated daily. Selling via non-traditional sources is a practice that's here to stay.

238.
Your Guarantee

What kind of guarantee, if any, do you offer your retailers? Let them know if you are guaranteeing:

➤ quality

➤ performance

➤ an exact match with the merchandise seen at the trade show

➤ a maintained markup of the merchandise

Guarantees have become commonplace within the consumer world and need to be as clearly understood in the wholesale world.

239.
Factory Outlets and Selling Direct On-line

Retailers need to know the same information about factory outlets as they do about discounters and mass merchants. They should be prepared to lose some of their retail customers when manufacturers choose to market merchandise in this manner. So let your retailers know if you have your own stores, and if so, where they are located and what type of merchandise they carry.

Sometimes your retailer's business can be hurt just by the name of the outlet. Even if it doesn't hurt them directly, it becomes an unnecessary annoyance. Inform your retailers. And don't forget to let them know of any upcoming plans to add a new outlet. Retailers must be able to make intelligent decisions about doing business with vendors they compete with.

240.
Know Who You Are

Have information readily accessible so the retailer can know exactly who the consumer is that your merchandise is targeting. Using either demographic or psychographic information, show your retailers where your product fits.

241.
How Can You Make it Easier?

The strongest and most loyal customers are the convenience customers. They remain loyal to businesses that are the most convenient for them. But convenience is more than location—it is an ease of doing business. It is also about saving time—not necessarily about saving money. How can you make yourself more convenient as a vendor to your retailers? Explore every aspect of your contact with your retailers to simplify and speed up the process.

242.
Know Your "A" Customers

Customers can be divided into three groups: those that spend a lot, those that order constantly, and those that recently did business with you. As a vendor, you need to know who these customers are and what category they represent. But the most important customers sometimes fall through the cracks. These are the steady, consistent, loyal customers who might not spend a lot of money, don't place a lot of reorders, or haven't placed an order for a few months. Yet your merchandise is always in their stores and their orders are placed on a consistent basis.

Know what your favorite type of customer is and decide how you value them.

243.
Bottom-line Resource: What Does it Mean?

Many vendors talk about being bottom-line resources—the resource that the retailer makes money with. But from the perspective of the smaller retailer, there seems to be more talk than concrete programs or promises.

Major stores can and do dictate to manufacturers the maintained markup they expect—or they will discontinue carrying the line. This forces the manufacturer to supply markdown money, additional advertising allowances, or off-price goods. It is time that these benefits are offered to the smaller retailers who are loyal accounts.

Formalize a guarantee maintained markup program and offer it to stores that qualify. The qualifications might include:

➤ approved computer systems

➤ minimum requirements of inventory

➤ advertising budgets

➤ store reputation

With such a program, a real benefit for you is the shift in focus from price to performance. This is a much healthier way to do business, and it creates a true vendor/retailer partnership.

244.
Call Center Courtesy

You spend money to employ the best salespeople, have a beautiful trade show booth, and produce the best possible merchandise. Maintain that high level of service by having the personnel who answer your telephones and communicate in other ways with your customers be well-trained, responsive—and compassionate. Even a slow-paying retailer deserves courtesy and respect.

245.
It is Not Bribery

What is an appropriate gift for a vendor to give a retailer? Most retailers are not looking for tangible gifts from a vendor. Their gift is quality service, promotions when available, and good follow-up. Most buyers do not like being put in the position of making decisions because someone has given them a nice gift. So send a thank you note for orders, or buy the staff a snack tray or candy assortment that everyone can share. These touches give the message that you appreciate doing business with them and are acknowledging the end of another year together—without trying to buy their business with a gift.

246.
How Many Bullets are in Your Holster? The Importance of Backup

Retailers make more money when they have the goods. The greatest deal in the world is worthless if a retailer has to wait a month to get the merchandise. To serve your retailers better, match the performance of the smaller regional vendor who competes successfully against much larger competitors by changing the playing field. Instead of focusing on price, they concentrate on "in stock" inventories that allow the retailer to place more "at once" orders.

The other industry where doing business with a stock house has always been an advantage has been the catalog business. Catalogs have always been more concerned with back-up inventory than having the goods available. With more and more retailers being forced into multi-platform retailing and a web presence, the vendor who has the merchandise readily available is becoming more valuable than before.

247.
Know When to Hold and When to Fold

No vendor can sell the world. Just as a retailer has to occasionally fire a customer, a vendor must maintain certain values and standards where anything less is unacceptable.

There are times when you must move on to the next retailer by saying to another retailer that we simply are not right for one another.

248.
Team Up–Join Forces with State Retail Associations

Every state has a state retailers association. Its goal is to improve retailing within the state. When the retailer's business is good, the vendor's business is generally good. These associations offer wonderful opportunities to meet and partner with retailers. All it takes is a phone call or e-mail to a state association to ask how you can be involved and what committees you can serve on. Becoming involved is the most effective way to network. It will make you stand apart because very few vendors get involved. The ones that do reap big rewards.

249.

Help Them Hire the Best

Finding good people is a struggle for most retailers. Help your retailers start the process with a job application form that reflects more effective content than most retailers have the time to develop themselves. Create a job application outline to illustrate the better questions to have on the application, such as:

➤ What special talents do you bring to our store?

➤ What do you see yourself doing six months from now?

➤ What was your biggest accomplishment at your last job?

➤ What would your last employer say about your work?

➤ If you could change one thing about your last job, what would it be?

➤ Why did you select our store as a place to apply for work?

250.
Is This Store for Sale?

Vendors can be the perfect conduit for bringing store buyers and sellers together. If a store is to be sold, it is in the vendor's best interest to see it sold to a retailer who does business with that vendor. Many stores have been sold to companies that have their own resources, causing a long-term account to be lost overnight because of new ownership. Try to be the matchmaker. It is to your advantage.

251.
The Last and Best Idea–Offer Category Management Consulting

The amount of data that computers offer to both vendors and retailers has created a whole new field of category management. Category managers analyze sales data so that every square foot of store space can be made to generate the maximum amount of sales and profit. A good category manager looks for inconsistencies among the percentage of floor space devoted to a product, the percentage of sales the product represents in relation to the total category, and the percentage of gross profit generated by the category. Ideally, each item should be in balance—if it takes up 10 percent of the floor space, it should account for at least 10 percent of the sales and 10 percent of the profits.

ABOUT THE AUTHOR

Rick Segel

 A seasoned retailer of 25 years, Rick Segel, CSP (Certified Speaking Professional), is an international award-winning speaker, author, trainer, and consultant who has delivered over 1,400 presentations on three continents and in 45 states. He is a contributing writer for numerous national and international publications and a founding member of the Retail Advisory Council for Johnson & Wales University, Providence, R.I. Rick is the Director of Retail Training for the Retailers Association of Massachusetts and the creator of the RAMAES, an awards program that honors outstanding Massachusetts retailers. He is also the on-line marketing expert for Staples.com.

Rick has authored five audio programs, two training videos, and three books. His most recent book, *Retail Business Kit for Dummies*, published by Wiley, became the #1 best-selling book about retailing in the United States in January 2002. *Laugh & Get Rich*, published by Specific House, has been critically acclaimed as a must-read for its insightful outlook at our entertainment-based society, and has been translated into Japanese, Chinese, and Korean. He has appeared on more than 100 radio and TV shows, including *Sally Jesse Raphael*.

For more information about Rick, you are invited to visit
www.ricksegel.com

LEARNING RESOURCES BY RICK SEGEL

AUDIO CASSETTES
How To Make Your Retail Business Profitable – This brand new 6 cassette audio program explores every aspect of the retail business. It uncovers the secrets to profitability and creates an easy to use step-by-step approach that can turn any store into a profit producing business entity. . . . $59.95

BOOKS
Retail Business Kit for Dummies – This 384 page book is the most complete guide to retailing today. It explores every aspect of the retail business and also includes a CD-ROM filled with forms, checklists, and guides to make retailing easier. $29.95

Laugh & Get Rich – This collection of tools and stories will serve as a blueprint for business success as it teaches you how to profit from humor in any business. It will show you ways to build stronger relationships, differentiate yourself from the competition, sell more, and keep more good employees...all with the use of humor! $19.95

VIDEOS
Effective Suggestive Selling—Did You See This? – This 60-minute video highlights an easy to use system that increases sales wherever it is used. It breaks the ice, facilitates multiple sales, and makes closing sales a simple. $49.95

Stop Losing Retail Sales – This 60-minute video is the perfect training video for sales personnel and their managers. It is comprised of short vignettes of do's and don'ts in customer service and sales. . . . $49.95

LEARNING SYSTEMS AND MANUALS
How to Run A Sale – This how-to, step-by-step manual reveals the secrets of the sale professionals and will increase your sales results significantly. $19.95

Open To Thrive – A revolutionary way to look at Open to Buy. It is comprised on an audio cassette and a tracker for sales, inventory, and cash flow. $29.95

ABOUT THE AUTHOR

Tom Shay

 Growing up in a family retail business, one whose various stores sold most everything found in a retail business today, author Tom Shay, CSP (Certified Speaking Professional), draws upon those years of experience in his work as a speaker and author. Since leaving front line retail, Tom has written over 250 articles on business management that appear in more than 55 trade magazines around the world. He is the author of *100 Profits+Plus Ideas*, a series of books published by Profits Plus Seminars that offer ideas for better promotion and management. He has also authored *EZ Cashflow*, published by Profits Plus Seminars, a book designed to help small business owners better manage the financial aspect of their businesses.

Since 1988, Tom has been speaking internationally to businesses in such wide-ranging industries as automotive, farm equipment, clothing, pharmaceuticals, hardware, lumber, floor coverings, professional golfing, bookselling, garden centers, sporting goods, pet shops, gift stores, and variety stores.

For more about Tom Shay, you are invited to visit
www.profitsplus.org

LEARNING RESOURCES BY TOM SHAY

BOOKS

Power Managing Ideas – Volumes 1 and 2 – Looking for ideas that can fast track your business to increased profitability? These books each have 100 tips from businesses that have mastered the short cuts to eliminating expenses as well as increase margins. . . . . $9.95 each

Power Promoting Ideas – Volumes 1 and 2 – Each of these books contain 100 tried and proven ideas for unique sales and promotions as well as ways that you can market to your customers on an individual basis. . . . . $9.95 each

EZ Cashflow – See your next 12 financials today. You can know your inventory and "cash on hand" well in advance so you can take advantage of opportunities and avoid the usual pitfalls of business. $28.95

INTERACTIVE TEACHING TOOLS

Relationship Selling Skills Card Game – Don't know what to say in a staff meeting when you are wanting to coach your employees toward better selling skills? This interactive card game will get the job done for you as your employees play a game of cards while actually sharing the techniques of master salespeople. $18.00

SOFTWARE

Power Promoting Screen Savers – A first and most unique tool for retailers. Designed for PC computers, these screen savers are sharing 100 pictures of displays from various types of stores. While viewing the display photos, you will also see the best of the promotion ideas from the two Power Promoting Ideas books. $18.00

Specific House Publishing
One Wheatland Street
Burlington, MA 01803

Specific House Publishing
Quick Order Form

How to Become the Preferred Vendor
251 Strategies for Doing More Business with Retailers!

 Fax orders: (781) 272-9996

 Phone orders: (781) 272-9995
Please have your credit card ready

 Postal orders: Specific House Publishing,
One Wheatland St., Burlington, MA 01803

Please send me _____ copies of *How to Become the Preferred Vendor* at $19.95 each, plus shipping and handling.

Name: _____

Address: _____

City: _____ State: _____ Zip: _____

Phone: _____

Email address: _____

Sales tax: Please add 5% for products shipped to Massachusetts addresses.

Shipping: US: $4 for the first book and $2 for each additional book. International: Based on ship-to location and current rates; please call for exact amounts.

Payment type: ❑ Check enclosed ❑ Credit card
❑ Visa ❑ Mastercard ❑ American Express

Credit card #: _____

Name on card: _____ exp date: ___ / ___

Please send more information on:
❑ Other books & learning products ❑ Speaking / seminars ❑ Consulting